Flight 2031

A Journey into Eternity

by

Dotty Larson

BLEST PRESS ▪ TEMECULA, CA

Published by BLEST PRESS

Library of Congress Cataloging in Publication Data

Larson, Dotty, 1924—

Flight 2031: A Journey into Eternity / Dotty Larson
252 pp.
Gospel According to John (NIV)
Reprinted by permission from Zondervan
1. Religion and Spirituality—Christianity—America

ISBN 978-0-9823380-0-1

"Through Dotty's spiritual gift of teaching the Gospel of John comes alive with personal illustrations from her life. The fresh insights of familiar Scripture will profoundly impact anyone investigating the claims of Christ. As I read *Flight 2031: A Journey into Eternity* my heart burned within me just as those men walking to Emmaus with Jesus when He *opened the Scriptures to them.*" (Luke 24)

Camilla L. Seabolt
Executive Director, Community Bible Study

"Dotty Larson's fine book is an invitation to light, truth, goodness and life...as seen in the person of Jesus Christ. Through her simple, yet profound analysis of the book of John, she takes us on a personal journey to find the real purpose for living. Will you accept her invitation to come and see for yourself?"

Luci Swindoll
Author and Speaker, Women of Faith

"Dotty Larson, my beloved friend for over three decades, has enriched the lives of thousands for 40 years with her gifted Bible teaching chock full of practical wisdom and golden nuggets of truth. Dotty is a good shepherd and mentor who will lead, guide, and encourage you as you journey with her through the pages of her book. You will gain valuable insights into your own life while learning about the life of Christ."

Ney Bailey
Author and Speaker, Campus Crusade for Christ

"In our relationship that spans more than thirty years, I've watched Dotty Larson closely and followed in the footsteps of her faith. I've watched her hold steady through the best of times and the worst and encouraged her to write about what she's learned. *Flight 2031* is her story; but it's not about her—it's all about Him. And the more I read, the more I know that what He's done for her, He'll do for me...and you."

Mary Graham
President, Women of Faith

Dedication

to my husband, Hav,
who steadfastly supported my desire to be used by God
and to my four children,
who patiently tolerated almost being "preacher's kids"

With a grateful heart to...

to all those people who eagerly study God's word
and have urged me to write a book that will help them
share that passion with those they love...

to Ralph Hetrick and Hal Lindsey, my first teachers,
who both encouraged me to learn
and to believe that I could teach...

to Tom and Emily Barton, my publisher and editor,
who encouraged me for years to believe that I could write
and for the immense contribution they made
to the book's actual production...

to Zondervan for permission to reprint the
gospel of John at the end of the book for the
convenience of the readers—especially those
who are new in their journey through God's Word...

to my daughter-in-law, Julie Davison-Larson, who
composed the music for the CD of this book. Her gift
of music has often brought me to tears, and I am grateful
that she wanted to use her amazing talent
to enrich the CD...

to my grandson, Robert Larson, who used his
incredible eye with a camera to provide the pictures
that add visual beauty and interest to this book.
May they help keep you turning the pages!
Our mutual desire is that they
will complement the text and thus help
communicate the message.

It has been fun for me to see my book become
a family project. I especially want
Julie and Robby to feel my love and gratitude.

Prelude

My Own Personal Journey

It has been said that "life begins at forty." I rejected that statement for years. Quite honestly, I liked being in my thirties. Those were happy years with my husband, fun years with our children, productive years in the community. I enjoyed playing tennis, showing off my great legs in that short skirt. I felt I had enough of the "wisdom of age" to make good decisions and still had enough of the "strength of youth" to carry them out. I had decided that thirty-nine was the place to stop. But life doesn't stop; the years roll by at an alarming rate, and I am now in my 80's.

I never worked outside my home except as a volunteer; I gave top priority to my family until my children were grown. Yet, when they left home, I never felt unfulfilled, useless, or depressed. I missed them—yes—but empty nest syndrome?—no. I went on happily, busily living my life primarily because when I was 40 years old I made a decision that completely changed my outlook on life and my attitude about my future.

I have survived the teenage years of four children raised in Southern California which surely didn't make it any easier. I have had my share of physical problems and suffered emotional stress in many forms—and now, I am dealing with the challenges of aging. I am painfully aware that well-advertised cosmetic preparations cannot keep my skin from aging indefinitely any more than well-publicized summit conferences can keep the world from warring incessantly. I have wrinkles, and, with two knees and one hip made of titanium, I am well on the way to becoming the bionic woman.

I remember well when synthetic fabrics lost their corner on the market and natural fabrics were suddenly "in." Cotton, linen, and silk materials all wrinkle, and fashion experts told us not to worry about the wrinkles as they proved our fabric was "real." I also remember when Mary, a young friend who was on the staff of Campus Crusade for Christ, told me she wasn't sure she was secure enough to wear wrinkles. But we all will "wear wrinkles"—and not just in our clothes—if we live long enough. Even Botox and plastic surgery have their limitations.

I have found that a relationship with Jesus Christ is the one thing that makes me secure enough to wear those inevitable wrinkles, walk with a cane, face the loss of my husband of 51 years, and deal with whatever life dishes out. And I am happy!

Studying the Bible has strengthened me and my faith. I have changed. I am both more tough and more tender. I laugh more easily; I cry more easily. When problems come—as they inevitably do—I have a resiliency that was once lacking. I can risk caring more for others without worrying about coming apart at the seams myself.

The change began when I became friends with the Jesus of the Bible. I had known Him for years but had never really devoted any time to fostering a friendship. I hope in this book, based on the gospel written by the Apostle John, I can introduce you to Him and convince you of the great advantage of having Him as your companion as you travel this road to eternity that we call life.

There is a complete copy of the Gospel of John in the back of this book—just in case you want to read the chapter in John that triggered the thinking for the corresponding chapter in my book. Also available is a CD of me reading this book.

I have included a short, simple prayer at the end of each chapter. Though you may not be used to praying, I urge you to read each prayer—out loud—if that doesn't make you feel too foolish. Even if you don't really mean—or understand—what you're saying, I would encourage you to do it anyway. In some inexplicable way, saying a prayer out loud to God begins to tune your heart and mind to receive a message from Him. My prayer is that He will get through to you—loud and clear!

Dotty Larson
Pacific Palisades, CA
March, 2009

Contents

Chapter 1

Time to Think

Chapter 1

Time to Think

I have always loved to travel and have had the great privilege of seeing many different parts of our beautiful world. One of my favorite trips was to Asia—Japan, the Philippines and Formosa. We spent four days in Taiwan with a charming young tour guide. She was attractive, intelligent, well-educated, and fluent in English. We enjoyed visiting with her as well as listening to her tell us about her country. Thus, we discovered her big ambition was to get off "this rock" as she called the small island on which she was born.

Toward the end of our time together she started asking us questions about our country, and the subject of religion was broached. On the way to the airport for our departing flight, she showed great interest in hearing about our Christian faith. Needless to say, I was frustrated about not having time to pursue that conversation. I explained Christianity to her as quickly and carefully as I could in the limited time I had. I will never forget her or the fact that as we walked across the tarmac to board our plane, I turned to see her standing behind the fence waving. I shouted back to her, "Read the Gospel of John, Stella. Read the Gospel of John."

This gospel is known and often referred to as "the gospel of belief." It was written by John the apostle—one of the original 12 disciples and a cousin of Jesus. It is his record of the life and death of Jesus Christ—a man who never traveled more than 80 miles from where He was born and yet has had a profound influence around the world for over 2,000 years.

Come and See

Jesus had another cousin, also named John, who was appointed by God to announce the entrance into the world of the Messiah, the long-awaited leader of the Jewish people. John the Baptist, as this cousin was known, declared, "I am the voice of one calling in the desert, 'Make straight the way for the Lord.'" (John

1:23) Jesus began His ministry soon after He was baptized by John in the Jordan River. Almost immediately He began to assemble a group of disciples, men devoted to Him.

John 1:29-31

29 The next day John saw Jesus coming toward him and said, "Look, the Lamb of God, who takes away the sin of the world!

30 This is the one I meant when I said, 'A man who comes after me has surpassed me because he was before me.'

31 I myself did not know him, but the reason I came baptizing with water was that he might be revealed to Israel."

John the Baptist did not fully comprehend that his cousin, whom he had undoubtedly known since they played together as children, was the promised Messiah until God revealed it to Him. Then God used him to reveal that fact to Israel.

The first two men Jesus called to follow Him were Andrew and Peter who responded to the prompting of John the Baptist and turned to follow Jesus, whose immediate response was to ask them what they were looking for. He had a way of making them think about what they were really seeking.

He still has that way about Him. Start looking at Jesus, and right up front you're challenged to look at yourself too. A little introspection is a healthy thing. The saying, "Know thyself," is an ancient one. Its origin has been ascribed to both Plato and Aristotle. As a philosopher that puts Jesus in pretty good company. The words He used were slightly different, but the meaning was much the same. When the first two disciples started following Jesus, He asked them, "What do you want?" He tried to make them think about their real reason for considering following Him and becoming His disciples. In other words, "Who are you and why are you following me?"

Start looking at Jesus, and right up front you're challenged to look at yourself too.

How long has it been since you stopped to take a long, hard look at yourself—inside yourself? Do you know your own strengths and weaknesses, your wants and needs, your goals? As of now, Rick Warren's book *The Purpose Driven Life* has sold over 15 million copies. Apparently a lot of people are anxious to know what their purpose in life is. Have you given any thought as to what your purpose is? Do you really know yourself? Are you even considering following Jesus? If so, do you know why? Why are you even reading this book? Is it because a good friend gave it to you?

John 1:43-46

43 The next day Jesus decided to leave for Galilee. Finding Philip, he said to him, "Follow me."

44 Philip, like Andrew and Peter, was from the town of Bethsaida.

45 Philip found Nathanael and told him, "We have found the one Moses wrote about in the Law, and about whom the prophets also wrote—Jesus of Nazareth, the son of Joseph."

46 "Nazareth! Can anything good come from there?" Nathanael asked. "Come and see," said Philip.

Being Found by Jesus

Jesus went out and found Philip. This is one of only three incidents involving Philip that are recorded in the Bible. He didn't particularly distinguish himself in any of them. Someone once said, "God must love the ordinary man; He made so many of them." Though there was **"God must love the ordinary man; He made so many of them."** nothing extraordinary about Philip, he did apparently have some good friends.

Andrew, Peter and Philip were all from Bethsaida up in northern Israel. In all probability, the two brothers, Andrew and Peter, had been talking to Jesus about their buddy from home, and that's why Jesus went out looking for him. Perhaps someone has been talking to Jesus about you…

When my grandmother died, I found my name written on her prayer list in the back of her Bible. My paternal grandmother was obviously ahead of her time because she wrote in her Bible, which was considered a desecration of God's word by most of her generation. They revered the Bible. Most of my generation still respect the Bible, but I'm afraid most of my grandchildren's generation ignores the Bible. It thrills me to know she talked to Jesus about me. One of the things that prompts me to look forward to going to heaven—that's the *ultimate* journey—is that I'll get to ask her some day what she prayed for me.

As soon as Philip decided to follow Jesus, he went looking for his friend Nathanael. He wanted to share the excitement he was feeling with someone he cared about. Nathanael was apparently well-to-do financially and well-endowed intellectually. Philip found him sitting under a fig tree. In the 1st century Jewish culture, "sitting under a fig tree" was virtually synonymous with thinking—often about spiritual things. People lived in small houses with poor ventilation—no mansions with air conditioning. It was cooler, quieter, and easier to think out under a tree.

We All Need Some "Fig Tree Time"

Do you ever wish you had time to just go out and sit under a tree? Do you ever feel like a little hamster running and running on a wheel until momentum has built to the point that even if you stopped running the wheel would keep on spinning? Our world is so geared to speed that there's hardly time to think. In *Future Shock*, a book popular in the 1980's and '90's, Toffler, the author, speaks of people who are "caught up in a new, stepped-up pace of life" who "live faster" than anyone else around. I have observed that if the pace does slow down, we quickly turn on the TV to fill the quiet moments. If I told a friend I couldn't have lunch because I had to have time to think, she'd think I was weird. A previously scheduled tennis game, another luncheon, a doctor's appointment, a meeting—those she'd understand.

But, we should not—must not—let life fly by without ever taking time to think about the significance of life. Too often we think of success, not significance. At the beginning of this first chapter, John tells us it is possible to be God's child. Most people today would tell you we are all God's children without giving it much thought, but John clearly states that some action is required. "Yet to all who received him, to those who believed in his name, he gave the right to become children of God." (John 1:12) Have you ever taken time to think about that?

Too often we think of success, not significance.

In Nathanael's day men had more leisure time than women. I don't think that's true today. My doctor confirms the generally-held opinion that more men than women have stress-related health problems, and, statistically, women do live longer than men. However, the prevailing idea that working outside the home validates us—confirms our value and our equality with men—has sent many women scurrying to the work place to prove their worth. Also, economic upheavals and soaring costs of higher education have made two income families a necessity for many. Hence, there are many overworked women who are trying to do it all—have a career and keep a marriage and family together. And there is a growing number of single mothers struggling alone to provide for their children's physical, educational and emotional needs.

> **There are many overworked women who are trying to do it all—have a career and keep a family together.**

In our homes we have work saving devices such as washing machines, clothes driers and dishwashers, but they are no longer enough. We "need" $200 machines to grate our cheese and chop our onions. Yet, no matter how many machines we have, theoretically to lighten our load, or how much "free time" we have wrangled from our work schedules, we seem to get busier and busier. Since nature hates a vacuum, something invariably rushes in to fill any void, any free time our machines or our bargaining power have bought for us. Our culture and our circumstances sometimes dictate our being overworked, but our frantic pace just may still be the result of too little self-discipline rather than too much work. That's my story.

There was a time in my life when I was so busy that if something was missing, I didn't have time to notice. If I had noticed, I wouldn't have had time to figure out what it was. Even if I had figured out what was missing, I wouldn't have had time to go looking for it—and I had done this to myself. I had four children and was productively, but not gainfully, employed outside my home. Though I never got paid, I was *very* busy with volunteer work. My problem was I had never learned to say "No!"

I was able to make my life work because I planned carefully. Since my husband and I were convinced that the family that plays together stays together we scheduled "play time" and our recreation of choice was skiing. Our four kids loved that.

Then one crisp, clear December day as I came swishing down a mountain in Sun Valley, Idaho, I caught the tip of one of my skis in someone else's sitzmark. This was definitely *not* on my schedule. However, God Himself had scheduled some "fig-tree time" for me. Eight months and two operations later, I finally got out of that cast so I could walk and drive the car again, but not before I did some serious thinking about my life.

Nathanael scheduled his time so that part of his day could be spent sitting and meditating on the things of God because he earnestly yearned to know Him. God had to knock me down!

Take Time to Listen

When Philip came to him, Nathanael wasn't satisfied just to share his friend's emotions. He had well-thought-out questions. He wanted answers. He was even prepared to argue. He knew the Scriptures predicted that the Messiah would be born in Bethlehem, not in Nazareth. What he didn't know was that Jesus was, in fact, born in Bethlehem. He actually knew quite a bit about the Scriptures, but he didn't know enough about Jesus.

He knew a little too much to be carried away by Philip's excited emotionalism; yet, he was not too hung up on his own superior intellect to be open minded. He was interested in what Philip said; was willing to hear him out. I am convinced that everyone is on a spiritual pilgrimage—*everyone*! Everyone's life journey is really a search for fulfillment and satisfaction. Sometimes we are completely unaware of our heart's restless searching. Nathanael was aware enough—sincere enough—in his search for God to agree to go see this Man. How easy it would have been for him to miss finding the truth because he was blinded by intellectual pride.

As an honor graduate from the University of Texas while still in my teens, I almost missed seeing the truth about Jesus because I was unwilling to take an honest, open look at Him as He is revealed in the Bible. You might say I was "too smart for my own good." Then I got married a week after graduation, had four children and became *very* involved in their activities and in volunteer work. My pride had found a powerful ally in my "busyness."

If God was trying to speak to me, I definitely was not listening. I am convinced that whenever God tries to speak to us through His Word, a book, or a friend, there are what Dr. Mark Bailey, president of Dallas Theological Seminary, calls "resistant dynamics" at work. When God is trying to communicate with us, the failure to do so does not lie with Him. Any attempted communication requires both delivering clarity of thought and speech on the part of the communicator and having an open mind and heart on the part of the receiver. God is an excellent communicator, which indicates to me that the problem is ours.

> **When God is trying to communicate with us, the failure to do so does not lie with Him.**

I think Nathanael was busy too, and he was certainly well-educated and intelligent. Nevertheless, he still noticed something was missing in his life. He took time to listen to his friend; he took time to think. His heart and mind were open; he wanted to understand. Way down deep he must have wished he had what his friend had; so, he decided to investigate.

On the other hand, his friend Philip knew he wasn't prepared for a big, intellectual argument. He probably felt ill-equipped and inadequate to present God's truth. However, he surely wanted to get his friend to come and see for himself. He just wanted to get him to really consider Jesus.

Are you willing to do that—to embark on a journey of exploration?

Take a Close Look

My brother-in-law once bought a fine camera with a close-up lens. Full of enthusiasm for his new toy, on a sunny summer day in Houston, he posed my sister against a brick wall in their atrium and snapped away. Back before digital cameras he had to wait for the pictures to be developed. When the prints finally came back, they looked exactly like her—you could see e-v-e-r-y-t-h-i-n-g! My sister is a beautiful woman; however, she was no longer a young woman. If he was going to use a close-up lens, it would have been kinder to use a softer light—and perhaps a filter as well.

Jesus has been around forever, but He doesn't need a filter. He can stand the very brightest light. The closest possible examination reveals no flaws. The closer you look at Him, the more you're going to like what you see. He is the perfect God-Man who came to satisfy the need for fulfillment and satisfaction of every woman—and incidentally every man—in this world.

Come and see...

O God,

Why do I think I have to understand everything before I get involved? I don't understand electricity, but I quite comfortably turn on the lights. Now I need spiritual insight; I am sort of in the dark about who Jesus really is. Will You enlighten my mind with Your truth? Thank You for the unanswered questions, the unsatisfied yearnings of my heart, the unmet needs in my life, the undeniable excitement of the "Philip" in my life. I am willing to take time to think. I am willing to come and see. Amen.

Chapter 2

A Miracle at a Wedding

Chapter 2

A Miracle at a Wedding

Soon after John the Baptist introduced Jesus to his followers as "the Lamb of God who takes away the sin of the world," (John 1:29) Jesus went to a wedding in the little town of Cana in Galilee.

At the wedding the host ran out of wine. Jesus' mother, who was fully aware of the power to work miracles that her Son possessed, sought to spare the host the embarrassment of such a faux pas. She asked Jesus to provide a solution to this social dilemma. Actually, she just told Him about the problem, assuming He would solve it. She seemed unaware of the timetable that controlled the actions of her Son. To honor her and the host, Jesus moved a bit ahead of His God-ordained schedule and performed the first sign of His public ministry—His first miracle. John refers to the miracles of Jesus as signs testifying to the deity of Christ and the reason for His coming into our world.

John 2:6-11

6 Nearby stood six stone water jars, the kind used by the Jews for ceremonial washing, each holding from twenty to thirty gallons.

7 Jesus said to the servants, "Fill the jars with water"; so they filled them to the brim.

8 Then he told them, "Now draw some out and take it to the master of the banquet." They did so,

9 and the master of the banquet tasted the water that had been turned into wine. He did not realize where it had come from, though the servants who had drawn the water knew. Then he called the bridegroom aside

10 and said, "Everyone brings out the choice wine first and then the cheaper wine after the guests have had too much to drink; but you have saved the best till now."

11 This, the first of his miraculous signs, Jesus performed at Cana in Galilee. He thus revealed his glory, and his disciples put their faith in him.

Jesus turned ordinary water into very fine wine, thus manifesting His glory. It has always seemed so right to me that Jesus' first miracle was turning water into wine. Perhaps that feels so right because it feels so wrong to me that Jesus is so often portrayed as a spoil-sport who really wants to turn your wine into water if you let Him into your life. I also love it that He honored the celebration of a marriage with that first miracle.

Believing Is More Than Seeing

It's interesting how many people today have been influenced by education or public opinion to doubt the validity of miracles. Webster's dictionary defines a miracle as "an event or effect that apparently contradicts known scientific law and is hence thought to be due to supernatural causes, *especially to an act of God*" (italics mine).

While much has been said regarding the so-called conflict between science and religion, there are many noted scientists who believe there is no such dichotomy. One such person was Dr. Victor F. Hess, discoverer of cosmic rays and winner of the Nobel Prize. Dr. Hess said, "I must confess that in all my years of research in physics and geophysics I have never found one instance in which scientific discovery was in conflict with religious faith." Then, with specific reference to miracles, Dr. Hess concluded, "Must a scientist doubt the reality of miracles? As a scientist, I answer emphatically: No. I can see no reason at all why Almighty God, Who created us and all things around us, should not suspend or change—if He finds it wise to do so—the natural average course of events."

While much has been said regarding the so-called conflict between science and religion, there are many noted scientists who believe there is no such dichotomy.

John sets out in his story of the life of Jesus to convince his audience that Jesus is indeed God, that He can suspend or change the natural, average course of events—that He is indeed a miracleworker. His miracles are signs of His deity. This first sign seems rather mundane, but a miracle it was. The water that was used for purification rites of the Jews now became such fine wine that the headwaiter questioned why it was served last. Since the guests had already drunk freely of inferior wine, they might fail to appreciate the superior quality. How many miracles go unnoticed in our own lives because we have had too many drinks of the inferior to be aware of how truly superior something that Jesus provides for us is.

I love the fact that Jesus chose for this first miracle to be almost playful, creating something that is symbolic of joy and celebration out of something so prosaic—and, doing so, to prevent His friend from suffering social embarrassment and simply to please His mother. What a gracious man He was! What a God of grace He is!

The Joy of a Miracle

One of the ways this chapter has always spoken to me is about how Jesus even cares about the comparatively unimportant things in life—like being embarrassed. I'm from Texas, not the deep South I grant you, but Southwesterners also have a "thing" about always serving inexhaustible amounts of sumptuous food. I still remember having a big dinner party at which I ran out of food. I thought I had made enough Chicken Tetrazinni for an army, but apparently it was too good or the guests were too hungry. I served buffet style, and they kept going back until I had to say, "Sorry, it's all gone." Jesus used my husband to remind me that nobody was actually still hungry and that I should be happy that they liked it so much. Do you have a tendency to look at the cup as half-empty instead of half-full? That's what I was doing. Jesus didn't fill my empty serving dish with more Tetrazzini, but He helped me relax and replaced my cup of embarrassment with a glass of joy.

> He helped me relax and replaced my cup of embarrassment with a glass of joy.

Judges 9:13 speaks of wine as cheering God and men, and sometimes wine is used as a symbol of joy. I seldom drink wine, but I often experience joy. I am grateful that I know that only God Himself can give me joy whether the circumstances of my life are merely embarrassing or actually devastating. I can—and often do—experience a deep-seated joy in spite of truly tragic circumstances—a genuine joy, though happiness evades me. Happiness depends on what's happening. Joy depends on our ability to handle what's happening. Our ability to handle what's happening depends on God. Happiness is a surface emotion; joy is a gut level emotion

Happiness depends on what's happening. Joy depends on our ability to handle what's happening.

that wells up from deep inside. It is based on the unshakeable knowledge that God is still in control and that He knows what He's doing. If you need a big dose of joy right now, it is available. As surely as Jesus was able to turn water into fine wine, He is still capable of doing miracles. He can turn your embarrassment or your heartbreak into a manageable emotion—even joy. He can give you a deep-seated confidence that you will be all right—that you can handle whatever He allows—with His help.

John 2:13-16

13   When it was almost time for the Jewish Passover, Jesus went up to Jerusalem.

14   In the temple courts he found men selling cattle, sheep and doves, and others sitting at tables exchanging money.

15   So he made a whip out of cords, and drove all from the temple area, both sheep and cattle; he scattered the coins of the money changers and overturned their tables.

16   To those who sold doves he said, "Get these out of here! How dare you turn my Father's house into a market!"

Trouble in the Temple

After the wedding, Jesus went from Cana down to Capernaum and on to Jerusalem where the Jewish Passover was about to be celebrated. In the Temple there He found merchants selling oxen, sheep and doves to be used for the obligatory sacrificial offerings. The money-changers were making exorbitant profits by charging for exchanging or converting the varied currencies into the required Hebrew coinage. This made Jesus really angry. He forcefully drove the animals out of the Temple and overturned the tables of the money changers and of those who were selling the doves. He said, "Get these out of here! How dare you turn my Father's house into a market!" (John 2:16)

In the 21st century, a typical reaction to this episode might be to suggest that Jesus should join an anger management group. But this was not an uncontrolled outburst, nor was it one in a series of frequent explosions. This was righteous indignation—not human rage. God's plan and purpose were being thwarted; God's character was being dishonored, besmirched. Sometimes I think we've lost the ability to be angry about the things we should be angry about. Where is our outrage over some of the things that are going on in our world that are diametrically opposed to God's plan and purpose and that defame God's character?

Does all this overturn your image of Jesus as a weak, passive, always peaceful man? First, we see Him salvaging a party by making wine, and now we see Him protecting worship by making a scene. Jesus was not as subdued a personality as some current teaching would lead you to believe. He loved a party; He enjoyed a good time; He did miraculous favors for a friend. Also, He loved to worship; He cherished a place dedicated to worship; He protected the practice of true worship with great zeal. After He drove the money-changers out of the Temple, the Jews demanded that He show them a sign to prove His authority to do what He had just done.

John 2:19-21

19 Jesus answered them, "Destroy this temple, and I will raise it again in three days."

20 The Jews replied, "It has taken forty-six years to build this temple, and you are going to raise it in three days?"

21 But the temple he had spoken of was his body.

At the end of this chapter—still early in His ministry—Jesus spoke of His own death and resurrection in veiled terms. Early in His ministry many of the Jewish people began to realize that He was indeed their long-awaited Messiah for "many believed in His name." (John 2:23)

Jesus came first and foremost to the Jews. However, He upset the status quo of their religious leaders. Consequently they opposed Him and discouraged their people from open-minded consideration of what He said and did as proof of who He was. Many of today's religious leaders do the same thing—and not just Jewish religious leaders, though they certainly still do. Joining them are many of the intellectuals—the educators—the scientists—even some seminary professors. It is disconcerting to have your preconceived notions questioned—your status quo threatened. But, if you want to know the truth, you have to be willing to consider even things that you previously rejected without much thought.

God,

I can usually handle things pretty well on my own. I guess that's why I don't always recognize my need for You. Thank You that I normally succeed in coping with my life. However, forgive me for my tendency to think that's because of who I am instead of who You are and who You made me to be. I want to be able to experience joy at a deep level in all the things that trouble me, not just the things that naturally delight me. Turn water into wine in my life—please! And help me keep an open mind, willing to consider new ideas that I have never thought seriously about before. Amen.

Chapter 3

Midnight Trip to the Obstetrician

Chapter 3

Midnight Trip to the Obstetrician

As the popularity of Jesus grew with the common people, the antagonism of the majority of the Jewish religious leaders also grew. However, there were exceptions. One such exception was a member of the Sanhedrin (the Supreme Court of Israel) named Nicodemus who came to talk to Jesus one night. It was during this discourse that Jesus spoke the words that have become so well known. Jesus said, "For God so loved the world that he gave his one and only Son, that whoever believes in him shall not perish but have eternal life." (John 3:16)

Did you perhaps go to Sunday School as a child and now think, "Oh, I remember memorizing that verse?" Or have you seen huge placards that say simply John 3:16 held up behind the goal posts at a televised football game and thought, "That's a Bible verse those crazy people are trying to get me to read?" Or have you wondered why In-N-Out Burger would print John 3:16 on the bottom of every beverage cup? Or is John 3:16 so unfamiliar to you that for all you know it's the ladies' room on the third floor at Macy's? Let's take a look at the chapter in the Bible where this verse appears.

John 3:1-3

1   Now there was a man of the Pharisees named Nicodemus, a member of the Jewish ruling council.
2   He came to Jesus at night and said, "Rabbi, we know you are a teacher who has come from God. For no one could perform the miraculous signs you are doing if God were not with him."
3   In reply Jesus declared, "I tell you the truth, no one can see the kingdom of God unless he is born again."

Chapter 3

When Were You Born?

Why is it that so many babies are born at night? All four of mine were. After the third midnight trip, I remember apologizing to my doctor for my poor timing. He assured me that I wasn't unique. Apparently, lots of births take place at night.

Dr. A. W. Tozer in his book, *Born after Midnight*, talks of the soul-searching which goes on far into the night as people grope their way toward God. Apparently, lots of spiritual births take place at night too. It happened that way with Nicodemus—when he was born the second time.

God Knows You Personally

Jesus is absolutely wonderful one-on-one. He knows exactly who you are and what you need. He knows your personality and background. He relates to each person individually—and that's good because we are so different. However, He recognizes that beneath the surface we are very much alike. God can see deeper than how you wear your hair or where you have it done, whether you shop at Nordstrom's and Neiman's or Target and K Mart.

Nicodemus could have shopped anywhere he wanted to for he was a wealthy man and a highly influential judge. He was evidently well-informed on current events for he had heard about this young Man from northern Israel striding into the Temple acting like He owned the place. Obviously, he had heard about the miracles Jesus was doing, and he never questioned that He had done them. Perhaps that's what stirred his curiosity and made him want to meet this Man for himself.

Appointment After Hours

Nicodemus came at night. There could have been many different reasons for that decision. Perhaps he was an introvert and didn't like the crowds which now constantly surrounded Jesus. He knew Jesus was considered a young radical, so maybe, as a Supreme Court member, he was unwilling to take the criticism which would almost surely result from their being seen together. On the other hand, Nicodemus may have just wanted a long, unin-

Late at night seems to be my best time for long, uninterrupted conversations with Jesus.

terrupted conversation with the Man. Late at night seems to be my best time for long, uninterrupted conversations with Jesus. I have heard it said that starting the day without prayer is like playing a violin concerto without tuning the strings. So, every morning I ask God to keep my spirit tuned to His Spirit, but my preferred time for long conversations with Jesus—and prayer is just that, conversing with God—is at night. I figure if He geared my body to be a night person, He'll be glad to talk with me at night.

Jesus seemed less concerned about *when* Nicodemus came than *why* he came. He took control of the conversation right away. He didn't even wait for Nicodemus to verbalize his reasons for coming—the questions to be answered or perhaps the needs to be met or the hurts to be healed. He cut through the pleasantries and spoke to the real issue: "Nicodemus," He said in effect, "you want to see the Kingdom of God; but you can't until you're born again."

Strange that Jesus would say that to Nicodemus, a political and religious leader. A wealthy man like that was probably a philanthropist or active as a community volunteer. The very fact that he was a Pharisee meant he prayed *seven* times a day. Did *he* need to be born again?

"Born Again" Then and Now

What do you think it means to be born again? A few years ago practically nobody, except perhaps Billy Graham, mentioned that term in conversation. Then it was used by prominent national publications, politicians, entertainment and sports figures to mention a few. In 2005, a Gallup Poll revealed that 42% of adult Americans claim to have been "born again." I doubt that public pressure to believe influenced their decision. In my opinion quite the contrary is true. In fact, other more recent polls reveal a significant decline in the number of people who profess to be true believers. Christians and their views and their right to influence public opinion are being marginalized very effectively by the mass media and the educational system in our country.

> Christians and their views and their right to influence public opinion are being marginalized.

We certainly know there was no peer pressure on Nicodemus to be born again. He was, in fact, probably the first person who ever even heard the term. When he did, he obviously didn't understand it because he said, "Surely he [a person] cannot enter a second time into his mother's womb."

Nicodemus had success but recognized that he was on a life search for significance. (John 3:4) Fortunately, Jesus can judge the heart attitude. He knew Nicodemus was not just being flippant. With all his material possessions and his influential position, he clearly was still not satisfied; Jesus was not the only one who saw that. Nicodemus knew himself well enough to see it too. He had success but recognized that he was on a life search for significance. Nicodemus was wise enough to recognize that there was a vast difference between success and significance.

Today, a person experiencing restlessness and discontent, in spite of having such possessions and position, might lie awake all night worrying and call a psychiatrist for an appointment in the morning. But Nicodemus came out in the middle of the night looking for Jesus. He didn't even wait until morning to see if the mood would pass. He sincerely wanted to make a fresh start in life, to see the Kingdom of God, to become a child of God. He was at a fork in the road. He was ready to try a new route as he sought to find significance. His own search may have been inspired by feeling that there had to be more to life than what he was experiencing.

Without a doubt, that feeling is responsible for a lot of the restlessness and lack of satisfaction that permeates our modern culture. That feeling—coupled with his curiosity about the young rabbi everybody was talking about—was probably what motivated him to go looking for Jesus. And Jesus told him about God's love gift to the world: you have only to "believe" in Jesus to be given this gift called "eternal life."

Does "eternal life" just mean life that never ends—a quantity of life—or is there also a quality of life that God bestows on anyone who believes? Jesus told this accomplished, prosperous citizen of the nation of Israel that He could provide citizenship in another kingdom—which at least implies a changed quality of life. If he wanted to be a citizen of the Kingdom of God, he must "believe in"—put his faith in—Jesus.

Though this is the first time the phrase "born again" is used, right at the beginning of his book in John 1:12, even before John had to dip his quill in ink a second time, he had written of becoming a "child of God." His assumption was that anyone reading his account believed that God existed and that it was possible for a human being to have a relationship with deity. He said that is accomplished by believing in the "name of Jesus." In biblical usage, "the name" of someone stands for the sum total of who that person is.

So John has now made it clear that to become a member of God's family or to become a citizen of God's Kingdom you must "believe" in Jesus—what He stood for and what He did. It is what He did that made it possible for God to exercise His justice and express His love without violating His character.

No matter how successful you are in the world's eyes, no matter how much people may think you "have arrived," Jesus says you cannot arrive in the Kingdom of God or be a child of God until you have been transformed by a process which He describes as being "born again."

The birth process is simple—but it may be painful—for God says you must ask Him to forgive you. That's a real blow to pride—that hurts. You must realize that you are not automatically His child. You must admit that you have made mistakes, that you have hurt others, that you have ignored Him. Then you must **To be forgiven by God the Father because of what Jesus the Son did on your behalf is to be born again.** ask Him to forgive you. He is waiting to forgive, but you *must* ask. To be forgiven by God the Father because of what Jesus the Son did on your behalf is to be born again.

To be "born again" is to "be saved." The term "saved" implies being saved *from* something, usually something bad. When a plane crashes we ask, "Was anyone saved?" When someone's home burns we ask, "Was anything saved?"

You Have to Be Born Again to Be "Delivered"

When I was born again, I was saved from lots of things. First, God saved me from myself! I come from a long line of "sensitive people." I ran true to form. When I was president of the Junior

Women's Club, I'd lie awake the night after the meeting wondering if I'd said "this" right, or what "she" meant by "that." Five years later when I was president of the Palisades Youth House Board and the Theta Alumnae Board, I was still lying awake rehashing the meetings. Some things improve with age, but age didn't seem to be helping me. I was too easily hurt, too easily offended, too concerned about what people thought of me. I didn't like being that way; I wished I could change. I even prayed I would. Then in that fateful fortieth year, I reconnected with God and things did begin to change. I started teaching a Bible study, but one day I realized I was still worrying about what people thought about me. In disgust at my own preoccupation with self, I cried out to God to change me!

Several months later I was *un-invited* to a luncheon. My friend who had invited me wanted some of her other friends to hear the featured speaker who was a Christian. She didn't want to come on too strong; she just wanted her friends to hear this speaker share the story of how God was working in her life. She told me that after more thought about her guest list, I might be a detriment to her plan because I was now a well-known Bible teacher. Of course, I said I understood; of course, I insisted I didn't mind.

I hung up the phone and sat there for a moment. I realized I had said all the "right" things. Then I realized I hadn't just *said* those things—I *meant* them! That's a big difference! At that moment I knew there was a *big* difference in me. I didn't even have my feelings hurt. I finally realized this was more about God than about me. He had been quietly at work in response to my heartfelt cry, delivering me from my genetic tendency toward hyper-sensitivity.

No Longer a Prisoner of the Past or a Victim of the Present

God can save us from both our inherited tendencies and our past experiences. Sometimes the past haunts, cripples, and controls the present. When you are born again, you don't have to be a prisoner of your past anymore. He can enable you to let go of your anger, your hurt feelings, the damage done by abuse, neglect and sometimes actual cruelty.

When I take a flight now I am struck by how many people are burdened by excessive amounts of luggage that they insist on keeping with them. I watch them struggle down the aisle, weighted down and slowed in their progress by the bags they drag behind them and the carry-ons they have over their shoulders. I feel for them as they try to find room in the overhead bins to store all their stuff. I think how much harder our travel through this life is because we seem unable to let go of a lot of things that have happened in the past that we are still dragging around. I wonder why we are so loathe to let go of all the unnecessary baggage that impedes our progress in this spiritual journey we call life. We can get help from counselors; there is surely nothing wrong with getting professional help. But we can—and should—also ask God to help us check a lot of old baggage and thank Him for losing it for us.

No matter how awful the stuff you are carrying around is, there is hope—there is healing. There is release and relief available. That is why Jesus is often referred to as "the great physician." Some soul scars may remain, but they need not cripple you.

Nor do you have to be a victim of your present. Your circumstances need not control your emotions. That should be welcome news to a lot of people. Valium was introduced in 1963 and by 1978 it was estimated that 20% of American women were taking it. In that year its use peaked, and Americans popped about 2.3 billion of those little yellow pills. Then Valium was joined by many other anti-anxiety meds. The National Institute on Drug Abuse estimates there are 2 to 3 million people who dangerously overuse those drugs. In addition, there are an estimated 10 million adult alcoholics in the United States. Over half of them use drugs also. Pain is part of life and for those who cannot handle it, tranquilizers and alcohol have become a way of life.

My mother used to have a plaque on her kitchen wall that read. "Anyone who can remain calm in the midst of all this confusion simply doesn't understand the situation." Apparently there are millions who do understand the situation, cannot remain calm, and resort to meds.

You don't have to be dumb, dense, or drugged to be calm, cool and collected.

But the statistics and kitchen graffiti notwithstanding, you don't have to be dumb, dense, or drugged to be calm, cool and collected. You can experience pressure and peace simultaneously! But before you can have that peace you want for the present, you must make peace with God for the past. Until then, you are condemned to live your life with all of its inescapable pressures—still haunted by failures in your past and without the resources you need to cope in the present. And the future will be no better!

No Longer Condemned

The final thing God delivers His children from is eternal separation from Himself. John 3:35-36 says: "The Father loves the Son and has placed everything in his hands. Whoever believes in the Son has eternal life, but whoever rejects the Son will not see life, for God's wrath remains on him." Talking about God's wrath is not very popular. We'd rather hear that God is love, and indeed He is. But He is also just and righteous—and the Judge who presides over all He created.

You see, the Bible teaches that Hell is an actual place—a place of condemnation, a place of separation, a place of fire. It doesn't teach that just in the Old Testament. Jesus Christ Himself talks about Hell—twice as much, in fact, as He talks about Heaven.

When I moved from Texas to the West Coast, I'd never experienced an earthquake—a tornado, yes—but not an earthquake. So, when I was awakened quite early one morning by a low rumble followed by a rolling motion that almost threw me out of bed, I was scared! I lay there trying not to panic. I watched the doors of the bedroom swing slowly shut. Then a little bisque figurine on my marble-topped dresser fell over and went all to pieces. I almost did too. I ran to check on the children; they had slept right through the whole thing—so had my husband.

I went back to bed and dropped off into a restless sleep. I dreamed that there was another earthquake. This time the doors didn't just swing shut; they jammed.

One day the doors to Heaven will swing shut and be jammed. There will be no way to get to God.

This time Susie and Larry didn't sleep through it. They were crying and calling me, and I couldn't get to them! I tried desperately to get that door open. Then I woke up in tears myself. I will never forget how I felt—the pain of being separated from my children when they needed me—the agony of being that close to someone you love and not being able to get to them.

One day the doors to Heaven will swing shut and be jammed. There will be no way to get to God. Too late the understanding of His love will be given to those shut out; too late the longing to return that love will be born in their hearts.

Wouldn't you hate to spend eternity forever wanting to get to God, yearning to be with Him, your heart burning with desire for Him? That, to me, is what the fires of Hell will be like.

Jesus Bought Our Ticket to Heaven

Jesus didn't want anybody to have to experience such pain and separation. I believe that's why He agreed to come to earth as a man to suffer and die for us. Now, we can be pardoned by God who is the righteous Judge of the world. Jesus paid our debt to God. That means you'll never have to "go to Hell." *People* may still say that to you, but *God* never will! God is concerned for you personally. He cares if your life now is "hell on earth." He also wants to prevent your experiencing Hell eternally. But He keeps His priorities straight. The temporal is important; the eternal is crucial.

You Have to Choose

The first time you were born you didn't have a choice. Your parents might have; but you did not. The second time around you *have* a choice—one only you can make. You have to choose to be born again.

God loves you so much that He gave His only Son to die for you so that if you choose to believe in Him, you will receive forgiveness and have eternal life. He only had one Son, and He asked him to die for you and for me. I have three sons, and I honestly can't think of anyone for whom I would ask one of them to die .

Have you ever stayed awake far into the night when the house was finally dark and quiet and thought about your relationships with other people and with God? Have you lost sleep you could not afford to lose, when being tired the next day would

> **God loves you so much that He gave His only Son to die for you so that if you choose to believe in Him, you will receive forgiveness and have eternal life.**

just make matters worse, wondering if it's possible to get your life straightened out? Do you really want to make a fresh start? Maybe yet another baby will be born after midnight.

Where are you in all of this—a little confused? Nicodemus was. He came to see a miracle worker, and he found a life changer; he came to see a teacher, and he found a doctor; he came to a classroom, and he found himself in a delivery room. And he was born again.

Dear God,

I am a little confused. I don't understand all this completely. Some of these words haven't been part of my vocabulary. "Born again," "saved," "Kingdom of God" are all new to me. But "mistakes" I know—I've made some, and "freedom" I know—I want to experience some. I have been dragging a lot of unnecessary baggage around. I'd like to check it and throw away the claim checks. I want to be free from myself, free from being crippled by my past, free from being powerless to cope with my present circumstances, free from the condemnation that I instinctively feel my future holds. I can hardly believe it's this simple. But God, I ask You right now to forgive me for my mistakes; forgive me for ignoring You for so long. I am glad that You are free to forgive me because I believe that Jesus died for me personally. I do believe that and now I am free. Thank You. Now I can call You Father, for I am Your child. Amen.

Chapter 4

Mid-day Trip to the Well

Chapter 4

Mid-day Trip to the Well

After Jesus' encounter with Nicodemus, He again left Judea for Galilee. The land of Israel was divided into three provinces; Samaria lay in the middle between Judea and Galilee. Almost 1,000 years earlier one of the great nations of antiquity, Assyria, had conquered Samaria. Their plan for control after conquest was to deport all of the able-bodied men and resettle the conquered land with men from other defeated nations. Intermarriage inevitably ensued. Prejudice against the resultant alloy of both race and religion led orthodox Jews to walk many extra miles to avoid Samaria and contact with the despised Samaritans.

Jesus Is Not Prejudiced

The shortest route back to Galilee ran through Samaria, but Jesus' choice of that route was not mere expediency. He made a deliberate decision to have contact with the Samaritans. He and His disciples must have left Judea by six in the morning to arrive at Jacob's well by noon. Jesus' concern over stepped-up persecution by Roman political leaders, stiffening rejection by Jewish religious leaders and the midnight encounter with Nicodemus undoubtedly compounded His physical fatigue from a long, hot walk. He was tired. The disciples went into town to pick up some 1st century fast food while He rested by the well.

An Unscheduled Appointment

Jesus relaxed, but only momentarily. He was about to have another unlikely encounter. He had met with a Jewish judge; now He was about to meet with a Samaritan woman.

What a tremendous contrast between that woman and Nicodemus! He could shop at Saks; she probably didn't even have enough money to shop at Wal-Mart. He was a strait-laced, upright man; she, by almost anybody's standards, was a loose woman. He was undoubtedly a social leader; her social acceptance was nil. He sought Jesus out; she just happened to meet Him at the well. Nicodemus was a serious, successful man on a search for spiritual fulfillment; he knew what he was looking for. She was a flippant, flamboyant woman trying to use physical satisfaction to meet a need she didn't understand. In short, he was a winner; she was a loser.

This poor woman had been married five times and was presently living with a man who would let her share his bed—but not his name. She didn't have much going

She was a flippant, flamboyant woman trying to use physical satisfaction to meet a need she didn't understand.

for her; she was a social outcast who had to draw water in the heat of the day, alone. She was a Samaritan; Jews didn't speak to Samaritans. She was a woman; teachers didn't speak to women. She was a social outcast; virtually no one spoke to a woman like her, except in derision. But Jesus saw her as a needy human being—an individual worthy of concern.

Jesus Is Not a Male Chauvinist

The original motivation for the feminist movement was to erase the inequities in the workplace and the exploitations of women. Ironically, Jesus has always looked at women with respect and treated them with equality. A woman is not a sex symbol to Him and never was. I'm sure He is for equal pay for equal work. In fact, this man Jesus has done more to elevate the position of women than any other person or organization that has ever existed.

This story of the Samaritan woman illustrates perfectly the attitude of Jesus. He has no bias toward people because of race, sex, social or economic position. In fact, in Galatians 3:28, the apostle Paul wrote, "There is neither Jew nor Greek, slave nor free, male nor female, for you are all one in Christ Jesus." The distinctions are not erased. There is individuality, but there is no discrimination. He welcomed women in His intimate group of followers and benefited greatly from their independent support of His ministry. Jesus treated every person He encountered as a worthwhile individual with legitimate needs to be met—and He still does.

The Need for Acceptance

One of the most basic human needs is acceptance which gives a person a sense of worth. Dr. James Dobson in his book, *What Wives Wish Their Husbands Knew About Women*, points out that men get their self worth from success in their jobs while women get theirs from success in their marriage and their home. Most women feel unfulfilled without a relationship with a man. We may not like to admit that, but it's generally how we are wired. This Samaritan woman was neither the first nor the last woman to run through a whole series of unsatisfying relationships hoping another person, another love would finally satisfy.

The divorce rate is down for the first time in many years. Sociologists theorize that the explanation lies in the high incidence of couples living together without contract. Therefore, when the relationship fails, they don't end up in a divorce court, but they do often end up in a psychiatrist's office. A temporary liaison can cause permanent scars. Victims of failed relationships will be forever changed; but divorce statistics will not change because the relationship failed.

The search for acceptance continues in the 21st century. This Samaritan woman tried to satisfy her craving with indiscriminate sex; some women still do. However, that's not the only thing we try. This insatiable search for satisfaction is as varied as people are. For instance, Jacquelyn Kennedy reportedly spent one and a quarter million dollars on clothes during her first year of marriage to Aristotle Onassis. The celebrity

> I didn't even realize I was searching for something until Jesus slowed me down enough to think about it.

bad girls whose escapades make the front page of today's newspapers have tried alcohol, drugs, sex, indecent exposure—you name it, they have tried it.

I tried community activities; I resigned from the boards of seven different service organizations when I broke my leg. I didn't even realize I was searching for something until Jesus slowed me down enough to think about it. Unlike the Samaritan woman, the things I did were socially acceptable. Even so, they needed to be evaluated for significance in the light of eternity. What was driving me? Was I striving for acceptance by my peers, by God, or was I subconsciously trying to stay so busy I wouldn't notice my own deep emptiness?

The Need for Accomplishment and Affection

In addition to acceptance, psychologists tell us we need both to feel a sense of accomplishment and to experience affection. A relationship with God can provide for all three of these basic needs. God accepts you; God loves you; and God offers you the opportunity to be of service to a needy world. We can—each one of us can—have those three basic needs met. But a relationship with God is a prerequisite. We must come to Him in the way He provides—recognizing we cannot choose our own path. We must not try to invent our own way to Him as the Samaritans did.

The Daily News

My grandmother lived to be 90 years old and had a strong influence on my life. I never understood her unusual exhortation to keep my behavior above reproach until I found out years after she died that her beautiful younger sister had been brutally murdered while still a very young woman. Consequently, my grandmother had to testify in court about the circumstances of her sister's life and death. Because a then prominent Texas politician was part of the story, my grandmother was subjected to reading a lot of character compromising details of her sister's life printed in newspapers all over the United States. She used to warn me, "Don't ever do anything you wouldn't want to see written up in the newspaper." So, I didn't!

When God began to reveal me to myself, I realized how self-righteous I was. What an insult to God, who is totally righteous, for me to think that I could be good enough to have a relationship with Him without coming to Him through Jesus, His established way.

For years, our family has enjoyed a home in the local mountains. I really enjoy the mountains when the leaves are changing color and falling. We used to have two long-haired cockers who loved to run through those fallen leaves and pine needles and then come flying back into the house. One day I was in the living room with the autumn sun streaming through a big picture window.

Henry, our little black Cocker, came tearing in to me, and, as I patted him, the sun highlighted the flying dust particles. That dirt was only visible to me because the bright sun light revealed it. The dirt in my life became visible to me only as God's Son's light revealed it. I am still in the process of cleaning up attitudes I never even saw as wrong.

Has He begun to reveal you to yourself? He'll tell you everything you've ever done and how He sees your life in the light of His total righteousness. Even if you've never done anything you'd be ashamed to see in the newspaper, I promise you, He'll point out mistakes. Only one perfect person who made *no* mistakes ever lived; His name is Jesus.

Ask the Right Questions

The Samaritan woman came to the well in the heat of the day to avoid contact with people; she certainly did not expect to find a man resting there. Jesus' encounter with this woman showcases His communication skills. Sensing her defensiveness, He asked her to draw Him a drink of water from the well; she was a bit surprised and disarmed. Then He piqued her curiosity—a good strategy to prolong an interview. He said, "If you knew **The key to spiritual growth is asking the right questions.** the gift of God and who it is that asks you for a drink, you would have asked him and he would have given you living water." (John 4:10) She was so intrigued that she started to ask questions, "Where can you get this living water? Are you greater than our father Jacob?" Dr. Martin Lloyd Jones in his book, *Spiritual Depression: Its Causes and Cures*, says the key to spiritual growth is asking the right questions. The Samaritan woman was asking some good ones, even though she was not a student of the Bible, and Jesus gave her a great answer.

John 4:13, 14

13 Jesus answered, "Everyone who drinks this water will be thirsty again,

14 but whoever drinks the water I give him will never thirst. Indeed, the water I give him will become in him a spring of water welling up to eternal life."

Do questions come to your mind? Ask them! Just verbalize what still puzzles you and expect God to begin to address your concerns and lead you to people or books that can help you find answers. He did that for me; He will surely do that for you also.

Pride and Prejudice

Because the Jews prided themselves on the purity of their religion, they refused to worship or fellowship with the Samaritans. When prejudice denied the Samaritans access to the Temple in Jerusalem, they built their own temple on Mt. Gerizim, assuming God would be pleased to accept their worship there. Ironically, we are still creating our own ways to relate to God—assuming that He will be pleased to accept them. Then, Samaritans, in order to protect their presupposition, had to discard any portion of Scripture that referred to Jerusalem as the Holy City or Mt. Zion as the Holy Mountain. With that criteria they were forced to forfeit the Psalms and the Prophets and all of the historical books. That left only the Pentateuch, the first five books of the Bible. Don't let your presuppositions force you to forfeit great blocks of Scripture. Be willing to explore them for yourself—then ask questions—talk to people you know who know the Bible. In other words, don't travel alone; try to find a good guide.

> Don't let your presuppositions force you to forfeit great blocks of Scripture.

I am glad Jesus knows when our search for Him is in earnest. Even when we have deprived ourselves of the guidebook, He will find ways to help us find the right road. He broke through the Samaritan woman's mindset and revealed Himself to her as the Messiah. He also revealed her to herself in the process.

The Truth Will Set You Free

When you know the truth, you are set free from preconceived notions that hold your thoughts captive. When you know Jesus, who is the personification of truth, you are set free from your past—sometimes quite dramatically. To be loved unconditionally is a freeing thing. The Samaritan woman momentarily forgot her necessary chores; she left her water jar and ran back to town. This woman who came to the well at noon to avoid people ran seeking those very same people to tell them about Jesus. The road to the well under the hot noonday sun may have seemed long and hard, but that same road, as she ran to tell others the good news, must have seemed short and easy.

She was free; she was no longer crippled by her past. It's exciting when there is an instantaneous change. This can happen because Jesus is a miracle worker, but usually He's a life-changer with a lot of patience. We tend to equate freedom with the Fourth of July; we expect firecrackers and skyrockets. We want to see spectacular signs that God is at work. But He usually works quietly and not too quickly.

However, He does work! And He sometimes uses unlikely people. Because this woman shared what Jesus had done for her, many of the Samaritans also turned to Him in faith. She did not have all the answers to questions they might ask of her, but she had experienced deliverance—she had enthusiasm—and she had joy! If you have experienced a change in your thinking about who Jesus is, have you told anyone yet? You don't have to know it all before you begin to share what you have found.

Are You Thirsty?

I am so grateful to Jesus for talking to both Nicodemus and the Samaritan woman; I see little glimpses of myself in both accounts. Like Nicodemus, I had my intellectual hang-ups. Like the Samaritans, I had thrown away great portions of Scripture—teaching that is vital to the Christian faith—because my "great mind" couldn't understand it. Like the woman at the well, I busily tried to find fulfillment—for me it was in my husband, my children, my home, my community service. But I was never completely satisfied; something was missing. Augustine, a philosopher and theologian of the 3rd century said, "Thou hast made us for Thyself, O God, and our hearts are restless until they find their rest in Thee." That was my experience.

> I had thrown away great portions of Scripture—teaching that is vital to the Christian faith—because my "great mind" couldn't understand it.

I have literally drunk from a dipper at Jacob's well in modern Israel. The well is deep and the water is cool. However, the day was hot and my relief was only temporary. In fact, I was thirsty again before I got back on the tour bus. I have drunk deeply from the living water Jesus offered the Samaritan woman. Oh, the joy of being satisfied!

Heavenly Father,

Thank You that the key to growth is asking the right questions—that it's all right to ask questions. Thank You for the skill with which Jesus deals with each of us. He told the Samaritan woman a lot of things about herself. Open my eyes so I can see myself, and open my eyes to spiritual things so I can see You. I realize the woman at the well lacked perfect understanding of the gift being offered, but she knew she was thirsty and wanted that water. With as much understanding as she had, she asked. You honored her honest request. I approach You now the same way. I, too, lack perfect understanding. I still have questions, but I am aware of an unmet need in my life. I am thirsty; please give me a drink of this living water so I can be satisfied. Guide me to Yourself! Amen.

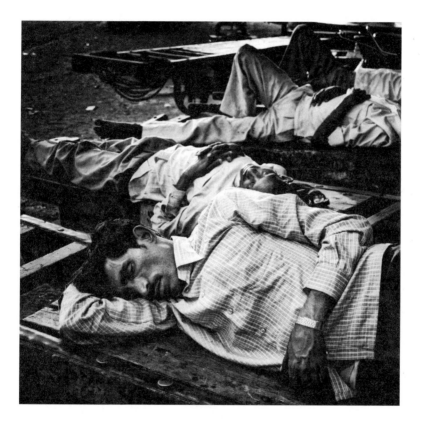

Chapter 5

Problems by the Pool

Chapter 5

Problems by the Pool

Our story continues with Jesus going from Galilee to Judea. Just imagine how many miles He walked on those hot, dusty roads. It was back in Jerusalem that He saw a man with a chronic illness that had afflicted him for 38 years.

John 5:6-8

6 When Jesus saw him lying there and learned that he had been in this condition for a long time, he asked him, "Do you want to get well?"

7 "Sir," the invalid replied, "I have no one to help me into the pool when the water is stirred. While I am trying to get in, someone else goes down ahead of me."

8 Then Jesus said to him, "Get up! Pick up your mat and walk."

Although He was back in town to celebrate a Jewish Feast Day, Jesus was always concerned with the needs of people. As He was walking through the town He came to a small pool called Bethesda that was believed to have healing power.

I have stood on the spot where Jesus stood that day—by that same pool. Intermittently, the waters are stirred by an underground spring. Jewish tradition in the 1st century held that an angel "troubled the waters" and the first person in the "stirred" water would be miraculously healed. The hope of healing brought hordes of sufferers to the pool. Jesus singled out one of them. I know He could have healed every one of those people. He can and does still perform miracles of physical as well as spiritual healing. Although He does heal every person who asks for spiritual healing, He does not heal every person who asks for physical healing. How He chooses whom He will physically heal remains a mystery to me.

Why Does God Allow Suffering?

Do *you* ever ask why God would allow so much suffering, so much heartbreak in the world? Is He without power so He cannot help? Is He without love so He will not help? Does He really care? Does He even know what's going on? The Bible teaches that originally the world was perfect, but deliberate rebellion against the known will of God brought death, disease, disaster. The cumulative effect of that is what we are now experiencing.

Years ago, our family went to Germany. At that time, before the Wall came down, a tour of West Berlin inevitably terminated there. From my vantage point, I could see the old National Cathedral of Germany in the background situated on the East side of the wall—the lower part partially obscured by that symbol of division and hate. From the bell tower a young East German soldier pointed his machine gun at us. I mentally noted the irony of such a use for a church, but it was our tour of East Berlin several days later that made the deepest impression.

That gorgeous old building, designed as a place of worship, lay in ruins; the stained glass windows were broken out; the interior had been gutted by fire and vandals; the landscaping now consisted of cracked cement and dead weeds. What had been a superbly executed fulfillment of an architect's magnificent plan had been destroyed. What had been a place designed for life and love and worship was a place of dust and death and war. The desolation seemed complete—not even a bird winged overhead. The young soldier stirred in his make-shift look-out post and broke my mood. But still I stood there wondering how the architect who designed that cathedral would have felt if he had seen it in that condition.

Our Shattered World

Suddenly it hit me! What must God feel when He sees what we have done to His magnificent creation? Our world is broken; so much of what God created lies in ruins. Water, air and even air waves are polluted. War, famine and disease plague us. He must let us make disastrous decisions and let us suffer the consequences. He created a cause and effect world. God can waive the rules; He can perform miracles;

We must reap the results of our choices or the freedom to choose has no meaning.

however, He does not routinely change the natural course of events. We must reap the results of our choices or the freedom to choose has no meaning.

The Old Testament is filled with stories that illustrate the principle that God blesses a life which is pleasing to Him and curses a life which is displeasing. In other words, though there are exceptions that disprove the rule, God usually rewards good behavior and punishes bad. In the Old Testament stories His blessing was usually health and wealth, and His punishment was illness and poverty and sometimes even death. The blessings and cursings were so visible it was hard to miss the message, and the Jews didn't miss it. However, they never made the transition in their minds from the illustration to the principle.

We are no better than they were. We, too, make mistakes in judgment. We fail to see that in the New Testament era material blessings and spiritual blessings are not necessarily synonymous. Furthermore, when punishment is not immediate we think it is not inevitable, and we often assume ill fortune to be the immediate result of personal sin.

Pay Now or Later

There are advantages in knowing that retribution will swiftly follow transgression. Prompt punishment is a powerful incentive to make right choices. However, though God's judgment is inevitable, it is not always immediate. Like shopping with a credit card, time lapse obscures the **God's judgment is inevitable; it is not always immediate.** price, but we still have to pay. Wrong behavior is still costly, and even the amount of the bill grows like interest accruing over time. We think we are getting away with drinking too much, smoking too much, eating too much, resenting too much, but we still have to pay. Anger and arsenic are both poison, and both can kill. Physical, spiritual and emotional health are all interrelated.

Apparently this man by the pool was paying the price in his own body for a recurring action or attitude because Jesus strongly implied that he was sick because he was sinning. The man thought he was sick because he did not have a friend to help him into the water. As long as he believed that, he did not have to accept personal responsibility for the untenable position he was in. As long as we believe someone else is responsible for our own situation, we can rationalize away the necessity of accepting responsibility and thus avoid our own accountability or liability. We definitely do need friends, but not to enable us to avoid being accountable to God for our own failure.

Do You Need a Friend?

Thirty-eight years is a long time to be without a friend. At the close of each of the first five days of creation, God said, "It is good." He was pleased with His work until the sixth day when He said, "It is *not* good for man to be alone." God knows our need for relationships; He programmed that need into us when He created us.

Nicodemus found a friend in Jesus. Jesus knew what he was thinking and spoke directly to his innermost needs. The Samaritan woman discovered a friend who totally accepted her; it changed her life. The man by the pool of Bethesda needed a friend. Most people do. Most of us have a lot of acquaintances but few real friends.

I have been blessed to have lots of really deep friendships in my life. One friend in particular, who has helped me for years with the Bible study I teach, has an uncanny, God-given ability to sense my moods and thus meet my needs without my ever verbalizing them.

A true friend meets your needs. I think it was the needs of this ailing, impotent man that drew Jesus to him. However, Jesus confronts as often as He comforts; a true friend does that. Jesus asked the man if he wanted to get well; a true friend says what you *need* to hear which is not necessarily what you *want* to hear.

Victim Mentality

The crippled man's response was filled with self pity. There is an epidemic of victim mentality in the 21st century: blame somebody—anybody—rather than accept responsibility. Blame your problems on what other people have or have not done. Play the victim.

Many feel that the root cause of the epidemic of depression that plagues our country and fills our doctors' offices is a direct result of the epidemic of victim mentality. Doctors' waiting rooms are flooded with patients who are filled with self-pity and who can barely function because they are so depressed. Some women are not even able to care for their small children as their responsibilities increase, and some are unable to adjust to their changing role of decreasing responsibilities as their children leave home. Too much to do, too little to do—drop out, cop out or have a glass of wine. So, not coincidentally, there is an alarming increase in alcoholism in women of all ages and stages.

Help!

Lots of people are admitting that they need help and are seeking it from different sources: Eastern religions, astrology, meditation, encounter groups. The god of Eastern religion is impersonal, uninvolved with human problems. Yet, I have seen tiny scraps of paper with written prayers tucked in a crack in the wall of a Buddhist Temple in Japan. The human heart needs a friend, craves a God who hears, who cares, who answers. How grateful I am that the God of the Bible is not an impersonal "First Cause." He cares.

> The human heart needs a friend, craves a God who hears, who cares, who answers.

Do you have a problem? Are you trying first one thing and then another to help you cope? Or are you trying to ignore what's troubling you—refusing to let it surface so you can deal with it? Enormous amounts of energy are spent suppressing problems. It's like trying to hold a beach ball under water. No wonder so many of us feel tired so much of the time. Sometimes it takes thirty-eight years to face reality. This man at the pool finally admitted he was helpless; his situation was hopeless. At least he was no longer in denial; he knew he needed help, and he asked the right person.

I'd Rather Do It Myself

Did you ever try to help a three-year-old put on his shoes and socks with him trying to kick you away with his left foot while he was trying to put his left shoe on his right foot? It's hard to watch a child struggle, but it is also hard to help until he admits he needs it. The admission of a problem is often the first step toward its solution. Jesus delights to help when you quit fighting Him, admit you have a problem and ask for the help He's been waiting to give you.

But, when you arrive at the point of admitting your need, you still have a choice to make and the options are too numerous to list. You can change psychiatrists, or chant, or meditate, or join another study group or service club. You can have a pity party; you can choose to blame other people for your problems. You can choose to remain an emotional cripple. You can rationalize that the whole problem is your husband's fault or your children's fault or your parents' fault. Or you can just admit your need and ask Jesus for help. A psychiatrist, a support group, a prayer partner—even a regular exercise program—can help, but in addition, you still also need the healing power that only Jesus can provide.

You Can Be Whole

Paul Tournier speaks to this problem in his book, *A Whole Person in a Broken World*. The world is "broken;" your body may be "broken;" your spirit or personality may be "broken;" but *you* can be *whole*—a complete person. The Apostle Paul in his letter to the Colossian church assured them that they were complete in Jesus. Colossians 2:9, 10 says, "For in Christ all the fullness of the Deity lives in bodily form, and you have been given fullness in Christ...." We have available to us the full power of Deity to be made whole—to be emotionally stable and spiritually strong—to have great coping skills.

We have available to us the full power of Deity to be made whole—to be emotionally stable and spiritually strong...

Babies Are Appealing—Or Are They?

When I was Susie's Girl Scout Leader, one of the mothers would never help. She got out of a lot of work by saying that children made her nervous. My son, Lance, has a colorful way of describing this attitude. He says a lot of people are *Intentional Babies*. He freely admits that he is one—sometimes. Intentional Babies like for everyone to have to tiptoe around their bad temper, their nervous reaction, their mood, their prima donna attitude. Would your husband be relieved of letting you spend money the family budget can't afford right now if you weren't an Intentional Baby? Would your children feel freer to bring their friends home if you weren't an Intentional Baby? Could your own friends relax and stop worrying about what they say and the way they say it if you weren't an Intentional Baby? Wouldn't you really rather be an adult? Wouldn't you like to be delivered from whatever is making you act like an infant—a victim?

You Can Be Whole—Now!

Jesus can deliver you. The world says, "You made your bed, now, lie in it." To the man at the pool, Jesus said "Get up! Pick up your bed and walk." He will make the same offer to you. The world says you are programmed by heredity, by your environment, even by the stars. But God says, "You are created in my image," and I am a decision-making God. You *do* have a choice; you *can* make a decision.

You cannot control what happens to you, but you absolutely *can* control how you respond to what happens. I like to say it is a question of will power. It is your *will* and God's *power.* By an act of your will you can **You can refuse to be a victim and choose to be a victor instead.** choose to claim the power of Almighty God. You can refuse to be a victim and choose to be a victor instead. Jesus did not tell the man to leave his bed there because he might need it again. He made no provision for a relapse.

Well, what are you waiting for? Are you still looking for someone else to blame for the mess you are in? What do you think has to happen before you can live victoriously? In other words, what is your pool at Bethesda, and who has to do what before you can experience the healing power that lies just beyond your reach? You can be a Christian *for years* and not ever get to take a victory lap if you choose to languish on your bed and cling to that victim mentality, suck your thumb and whine. Or you can get up and go for a walk, give your life a thumb's up and vow to think of what you have rather than whine about what you don't have.

Attitude is everything!

Dear Father God,

I don't want to be born again but never grow up. I don't want You to grieve over me as another one of Your children who is developmentally challenged. I don't want to be an Intentional Baby. I don't want to see myself as a victim. By an act of my will, I claim Your power to be a well-adjusted person in spite of my past or my present circumstances. Please let me see a change in myself to encourage me to believe that You are at work in my life. Help me move on down the road toward maturity. Thank You for being my Friend in the midst of my imperfection and my need. Amen.

Chapter 6

Picnic by the Sea

Chapter 6

Picnic by the Sea

The religious leaders were upset when Jesus healed the man by the pool of Bethesda on the Sabbath. Their observance of the command God had given them to set aside a day for rest and worship had been expanded to such an extreme that they felt Jesus had broken a law of God when He healed the crippled man. Jesus' defense of His right to work on the Sabbath was going too far. They understood He was making Himself equal with God; so they decided to kill Him. What an unbelievable approach for religious leaders to take! But it was expedient to get rid of Jesus. Once a course of action is determined by simple expediency, what is to prevent achieving the goal in the simplest possible way?

God's Timetable

Jesus was aware of His Father's scheduled plan for His life, so He returned to Galilee to avoid premature arrest or death. There no religious hierarchy would attack Him, and there He was near family and boyhood friends. Temporarily, He was safe.

He had been a private person, adept at personal conversation, skilled at training the small band of men who were His followers. Now into His third year of ministry, He had become a public figure, addressing thousands, surrounded by masses of people. The last six months of His life He was constantly embroiled in confrontation, controversy and crowd control. He had performed so many miracles that multitudes followed Him. There was excitement in the air; *He* was where the action was. The crowds sensed there was something in it for them, but they were unclear about what that was. They were too materialistic—their minds too earthbound—to comprehend the spiritual benefits He could give.

Jesus had that trouble throughout all three years of His ministry and with all different kinds of people. From Nicodemus' remark about re-entering his mother's womb to the Samaritan woman's request for the promised water so she wouldn't have to keep returning to the well, people failed to grasp the spiritual significance of what He said or did. The miracles He performed were meant to be signs to prove that He was the long-expected Messiah, but most people just didn't have a clue. They almost all failed to grasp the spiritual significance of what He said or did.

Anybody for a Picnic?

One beautiful spring day a throng of people followed Him out to the shores of the Sea of Galilee. About 5,000 men and an undetermined number of women and children waited for hours while He went up on the hillside to be alone with His disciples. Perhaps the children played games in the meadow or waded in the shallow water near the shore of the lake. The women probably sat quietly in what shade they could find and visited. The men undoubtedly added to the warmth of the day with heated discussions about the repercussions of following this Man. As the day waned, Jesus came back down the mountain; the crowd surged toward Him.

He didn't want to be followed as a miracle-worker who could heal the sick, provide material benefits and lead a victorious military campaign against Rome. Those things, of course, were exactly what the people wanted from Him. Yet, He looked on them as sheep without a shepherd and felt compassion. A shepherd provides his flock with direction, protection—and food. So, Jesus asked Philip where they could buy bread.

Philip assessed the situation and expressed the perfectly logical thought that they couldn't afford to provide food for that crowd. So, Jesus accepted five small barley loaves and two little fish from a generous young lad. Miraculously, He multiplied that little boy's lunch until it was sufficient to feed thousands of people—and there were leftovers. The men quickly grasped the significance of having a leader who could provide such material abundance. There was no government aid program in those days, but the idea of being provided for has universal appeal. They tried to seize Him and force Him to be their King.

> There was no government aid program in those days, but the idea of being provided for had universal appeal.

John 6:26, 27

26 Jesus answered, "I tell you the truth, you are looking for me, not because you saw miraculous signs but because you ate the loaves and had your fill.

27 Do not work for food that spoils, but for food that endures to eternal life, which the Son of Man will give you. On him God the Father has placed his seal of approval."

The Man Who Would NOT Be King

How many of us try to use Jesus to satisfy our own materialistic desires? Perhaps you have heard about the abundant life, and you think that sounds like money and trips and a bigger clothes budget, and you'd like that. Fortunately for us, Jesus actually allows Himself to be found by people with no more understanding of His true mission than those Galilean picnickers.

He is concerned when we're hungry. He cares when we hurt, physically or emotionally, but He cares most of all about spiritual pain, separation and deprivation. He wants us to know the Father. He does not want to see us separated from God.

If only we could grasp how infinitely more important spiritual healing is than physical healing. If only we could comprehend how much more important it is to be fed spiritually than **Jesus can satisfy spiritual hunger at the deepest level.** it is to be fed physically. If only we yearned to be clothed in robes of righteousness and not designer duds. The most important purpose of the miracle of the fish and loaves was not to satisfy the physical hunger pangs of that crowd but to point them to the truth that Jesus can satisfy spiritual hunger at the deepest level.

Embedded in the story of the feeding of the 5,000 is the pronouncement made by Jesus that He is the Bread of Life. Taken literally, His claim that anyone who believes in Him will never be hungry or thirsty again is obviously not true. Many of God's most devoted servants have suffered physical deprivation. Jesus was claiming the ability to satisfy the deepest spiritual human need and longing. That is indisputably true. Bread is a very basic element of physical sustenance; Jesus is the absolute essential element of spiritual sustenance. He is the Bread of Life.

Our world is much like theirs was. Rome in its heyday was a hedonistic society. Overindulgence in food, drink and sex was a way of life. A frenetic drive for fulfillment drove them to offensive excesses in things that can never truly satisfy. Ours, like theirs, is also a materialistic society—if you can't touch it, taste it, smell it, see it, hear it, or spend it, it's not real. How often we too are driven to offensive excesses. How wrong they were! How wrong we are!

Fill Up on Bread

If only we sought to satisfy our spiritual needs as diligently as we do our physical needs. Truthfully, we must think the physical more important than the spiritual—this world more important than the next. We are more worried about whether our children take their vitamins than whether they ever own or read a Bible. We are more concerned over which college or university they are admitted to than whether they are ever admitted to Heaven. We sense there has to be more to life than what we are experiencing. We hunger for something more, but we don't know how to find it or how to direct our children to it. Too often we just continue to try to fill that void with material things.

Sometimes I suspect we do a little psychological substitution trying to satisfy spiritual hunger by physical overeating. I believe that at least partially explains the enormous number of overweight people in the United States. Obviously, the need of this crowd of Galileans went deeper than having bread to eat—and so does ours!

> **Sometimes I suspect we do a little psychological substitution trying to satisfy spiritual hunger by physical overeating.**

God Planned Ahead

God was orderly and consistent in His creation. When He created lungs, He had already created air to breathe. When He created eyes, He had already created beauty to appreciate. When He created tummies, He had already provided all the ingredients for hamburgers, brownies and ice cream sundaes. Logically, it follows that when He created us with spiritual hunger, He had already planned to satisfy us with Himself. Blaise Pascal, the famous French physicist and theological philosopher of the 17th century wrote: "There is a God-shaped vacuum in the heart of every man that cannot be filled by any created thing but can only be filled by God the Creator Himself."

Hide and Go Seek

After the picnic He had provided, Jesus sent His disciples to the other side of the lake in the only available boat. Then He single-handedly defused the explosion of that unruly mob which sought to force Him into a role He refused to play. He went up on the mountain to pray. Hours later when He chose to join His disciples, He did another pretty spectacular thing. He walked on water.

The Sea of Galilee is a deep lake, and it can be treacherous when it is as windy as it was that night. His disciples had struggled to make progress in the rough waves for over three hours. They had not yet comprehended that as God He even had control over the elements of nature. They were terrified when they saw Him coming across the lake toward them—walking on that churning water. After He reassured them, Jesus got in the boat, and they arrived safely at the shore they were trying to reach.

The next morning the crowd went looking for Jesus again. They didn't know exactly where He was, but they knew where His disciples were. Study the strategy of those 1st century seekers if you're looking for Jesus. Find a group of His followers, and they should be able to tell you how to find Him. That still unsatisfied crowd found Jesus among His disciples, and He started to teach them again.

Hey, Mom, I Don't Have Anything to Do

Jesus said, "Do not work for food that spoils, but for food that endures to eternal life, which the Son of Man will give you." (John 6:27) "How do you work for this eternally satisfying food?" they asked. "What must we do to do the works God requires?" (John 6:28)

Must I go to church every Sunday morning? How often must I offer to work in the kitchen for church dinners? How many aprons must I make for the church bazaar or how many pounds of fudge? Would continuing my work in the Charity League be just as good? How much money must I give to the church? Could I give to the

United Fund instead? Does caring for my elderly mother count for anything? What about my sick neighbor? I've never taught Sunday School, but I'm a Cub Scout den mother; will that do? What must I do to work the work of God? Jesus answered, "The work of God is this: to believe in the one he has sent." (John 6:29)

For years I have regularly flown to Texas to see family. I make a reservation; I pack a bag; and I go to the airport. Why? Because I believe that the plane will take me to see my son and his precious family, my sister, and my dearly loved nieces. In the biblical sense of the word, if I *really* believe—if I have faith—I'll board the plane. I can't work hard enough to get there; flapping my arms won't help at all! In other words, a lot of outward show of activity won't accomplish a thing. But that plane will take me there if I believe enough to act on what I say I believe—if I cast myself totally on its ability to deliver me to my destination. And so can Jesus deliver me—deliver you—to Heaven itself, and the good news is that the ticket is free. You don't have to work to earn it.

God's Duty Roster

Once you're on your way, God provides good things for you to do while you travel. Just as we try to keep young children occupied while on a plane so they won't want to aimlessly run up and down the aisle getting in the way of flight attendants who have work to do, God plans ahead what He'll have us occupied with so we won't annoy or impede the work performance of other travelers. Ephesians 2:8-10 says: "For it is by grace you have been saved, through faith—and this not from yourselves, it is the gift of God—not by works, so that no one can boast. For we are God's workmanship, created in Christ Jesus to do good works, which God prepared in advance for us to do."

> **"We are God's workmanship, created in Christ Jesus to do good works, which God prepared in advance for us to do."**

I graduated from college with a major in English literature which allowed me to indulge my love of poetry. I'm fascinated by the fact that in the original language that verse says "for we are God's poem…" To me that means that there is rhyme and reason and rhythm to our lives when we do the things God created us to

do. Good poetry is beautiful, and you can be sure God didn't com-
pose any bad poems. It's only when we get out of sync with Him
that the beauty and goodness are
lost. It is certainly not that what you
do is unimportant; it's just that you
have to believe *first*, and work for

> You become God's child by
> faith; then, all God's children
> have pre-assigned chores.

God *second*. The sequence is the key. You become God's child by
faith; then, all God's children have pre-assigned chores. God will
tell us what He created us and equipped us to do if we are willing
to listen to Him with open hearts and minds and if our deliberate
purpose is to obey Him. Once we realize how much He loves us,
we will be eager to respond by doing the job He has for us, and our
lives will reflect His beauty.

A Tug of War: the World vs. the Lord

Jesus continued to teach the people that only He could give
satisfaction, only He could fill the longing in their hearts. The
world can tease and tantalize you, holding out hope that just one
more thing will finally bring satisfaction. Jesus came to tell us that
God alone can truly satisfy. Jesus even told them that He knew that
the world was so enticing that they would never come to Him and
receive eternal life, eternal joy, eternal satisfaction unless the Father
Himself drew them to Him.

In another book John wrote, he urged his readers not to love
the world or anything in it because the world and its desires will
not last. However, he says that the person who does the will of
God *will* last forever—will live forever in the presence of God
whom he faithfully serves.

I'm sure each of us has watched at least one launching of a
space flight. How carefully the plans are made—each detail
checked, the exact moment for blast off precisely determined by
scientific calculations beyond my grasp. Those calculations are
based on the absolute dependability of the movement of the stars
and planets which follow a precise pattern. I have sat with my heart
in my throat, awestruck at the tremendous thrust of power those
rockets provide for the space ship's escape from the earth's mag-
netic tug as it launches out into space. How reassuring it is to me
that the awesome power of God pulled me away from the world's

grasp and into orbit around Jesus. There are no accidents or miscalculations in God's plan. No re-scheduling is ever required because of bad weather. His timing is perfect; His power is sufficient. But you have to want the satisfaction only He can give enough to release your hold on the world and hold on to God like your life depended on it...because it does.

Dear Father,

I have tried to live a good life and there are times when I really feel satisfied with my life just the way it is—but not always. For a lot of years, I've been tied to this world. I know You wouldn't approve of my neglecting my responsibilities, and I don't want to. But I don't want to be dependent on what this world offers for my ultimate satisfaction. I have tried that, and I'm still not completely satisfied. I am ready for Blast-Off! I'm a little frightened of what this trip involves, but I'm ready to take a chance. Take me at my word, and let's "go for it." What a trip this is going to be. Amen.

Chapter 7

Teacher of the Year

Chapter 7

Teacher of the Year

Great teachers are rare. They are the ones who hold the attention, challenge the mind, and capture the imagination so the student is excited about learning and wants to learn more. Have you ever had a teacher like that? I had a teacher in the seventh grade I'll never forget. He made me want to learn and go on learning.

Jesus was such a teacher. He was entertaining, inspiring, and knowledgeable about His subject. By the time we read this account of an incident in His highly controversial teaching career, He had almost three years' experience under his belt.

John 7:16-17

16 Jesus answered, "My teaching is not my own. It comes from him who sent me.
17 If anyone chooses to do God's will, he will find out whether my teaching comes from God or whether I speak on my own...."

A Little History Review

John's book gives us carefully selected details which usually do not duplicate the accounts of Jesus' life previously written by Matthew, Mark and Luke. His gospel concentrates on the parts of Jesus' life story that John felt needed additional embellishment, revelation, or emphasis. His account deals primarily with the first and last six months of Jesus' ministry. It was during the latter six months that His healing of the crippled man at the pool of Bethesda so infuriated the Jewish religious leaders that His life was in jeopardy. As a consequence, He had returned to Galilee where He was safer and had remained in that area.

Jerusalem Becomes a Giant Campground

It was the time of the Feast of Tabernacles, a divinely appointed feast designed by God as a strong reminder of His protection and provision during the Israelites' exodus through the Sinai Desert. (See Exodus 13:20-22) God added significance to the festival by telling them to celebrate it after the harvest. This Feast, therefore, had agricultural, historical, and religious significance. Imagine our Thanksgiving, July 4th, and Easter all rolled into one.

For eight days pilgrims in the city for the celebration, and even the regular residents, lived in shelters made of palm fronds and tree branches. Jerusalem became a giant camp ground in a festive mood. Every morning for seven days the priest moved at the head of a procession of worshippers to the pool of Siloam where they filled golden water pots. Back at the temple, as part of a well-ordered but exuberant ritual, they poured the water on the altar of God to commemorate God's provision of water in the desert. Every evening they lit candles in remembrance of the pillar of fire that had led them by night through the desert. Josephus, the 1st century Jewish historian, stated that if you had not participated in this Feast, you had never experienced true joy.

Family Pressure

Jesus enjoyed life; good friends and parties were important to Him. However, it was not fear of missing a party that drew Him back to Jerusalem. Nor did He go because His brothers urged Him to be seen there to further His career. He never lent even tacit approval to that reason for attending a religious meeting.

The attitude of His brothers amazes me; they did not yet believe in Him. They had grown up in the same house with Him; so it's inconceivable to me that they didn't know that He was a unique person. Obviously, they knew He could work miracles, and yet they persisted in their unbelief. Perhaps, much like children who have been taken to church since before they could walk or talk, they had been constantly exposed to Jesus but never confronted by Jesus. Half

Perhaps, much like children who have been taken to church since before they could walk or talk, they had been constantly exposed to Jesus but never confronted by Jesus.

jesting, half contemptuous, half believing, they exhorted Him to show His hand. (John 7:3-5)

Close Only Counts in Horseshoes

It's not good enough to be half convinced; it's not good enough to be almost persuaded; it's not good enough to be close to believing that Jesus is God. You either believe it or you don't.

You would think if anybody could be born automatically into the family of God these brothers could. But each person born physically into the family of man must choose to be born spiritually into the family of God. It doesn't matter who your brothers or your cousins are or who your mother or your grandmother is or what they believe. Like entering a huge stadium, we have to hold our own ticket of faith and go through that turnstile alone. The only exception—a baby too young to walk through on his own. Jesus' brothers were grown men, and they didn't have the right ticket. Jesus said in essence, "If you're not for me, you're against me." (Matthew 12:30) And his brothers were not for Him, except perhaps for the personal benefits that might accrue if He actually turned out to be the Messiah.

Jesus refused to yield to their pressure to attend the Feast with them. Had He done so, the religious leaders would have arrested Him before the eighth day when He planned to publicly present Himself in the Temple.

A Feast of Controversy

After His family left for the Feast, Jesus did go to Jerusalem. He slipped quietly into town and found everybody talking about Him. Some said, "He is a good man." Others replied, "No, he deceives the people." (John 7:12) Nobody likes to be the target of a whispering campaign; nobody enjoys being embroiled in controversy. However, that did not deter Him from His course. He arrived about midway through the Feast and went to the Temple to teach. The leaders of the Jews marveled at this uneducated man from Galilee teaching with such knowledge and finesse.

It is fairly common today to be "put down" by someone who implies that if you're really smart or well-educated you won't be impressed with Jesus and His Word. Those Judean Jews were proven leaders with the finest education available, and Judea was the cultural, economic, and educational center of the country. Yet, they were impressed. He has impressed others down through the centuries: Bach, Galileo, Joan of Arc, Michelangelo, Handel, Marie Curie, Columbus, Sir Isaac Newton, Florence Nightingale, Elizabeth Barrett Browning, William Gladstone, Abraham Lincoln, Helen Keller, Werner von Braun. From every field of endeavor in every century, there have been outstanding people who were impressed with this Man. Napoleon Bonaparte said, "I know men and Jesus Christ was no mere man."

Jesus May Multiply Loaves, but He Divides People

Jesus never claimed to be a self-made, self-taught man. When He was asked where His wonderful teaching came from, He said it came from God. Then He made an even more startling statement. In essence He said that if they did not accept and believe His teaching their problem was not intellectual but moral. He told them if they were willing to do God's will, they would know whether or not His teaching was from God.

Jesus had a way of polarizing opinion about Himself. There was no middle ground.

That's a sure-fire test. It should not be taken lightly. You can know if Jesus is God; you can know if the Bible is true—but only if you are willing to obey God when He makes His will known to you. No wonder He caused division everywhere He went. Jesus had a way of polarizing opinion about Himself. There was no middle ground.

A Multiple Choice Test

People still debate today. Was Jesus a good man or did He deceive the people? Because of the high moral and ethical quality of His teaching, many prefer to say He was a great teacher but was Himself somehow deceived into thinking He was co-equal with God. We do not have the option of simply saying He was a great teacher and a good man. He was either a great deal more or a great deal less. C. S. Lewis elucidates this idea in *Mere Christianity*. If Jesus said He was God and He was not and He knew He was not, He was a deceiver, a liar. If He said He was God and He was not but He did not know He was not, then He was a madman, a lunatic. There is a third alternative. If He said He was God and He *was* God, then He *is* truly Lord. Lunatic, liar, Lord—take your pick—those are your only options.

If you refuse to choose, you have chosen already. There was once a jailer from Philippi who asked the apostle Paul, "What must I do to be saved?" Paul replied, "Believe in the Lord Jesus and you will be saved...." (Acts 16:30, 31) If you asked what you must do *not* to be saved, the answer is simple—absolutely nothing!

God Doesn't Grade on the Curve

How well I remember a time when I didn't understand that to choose not to make a decision was to have made one. I believed in God and His Heaven all right, but I did not know I had to make ONE all-important choice that determined whether He'd admit me when I arrived there. I thought Billy Graham was proud and presumptuous because he said he knew he was going to Heaven when he died. I thought my acceptance would be based on my performance. I assumed my scores were to be compared to those of other applicants; I had always done well on exams. I figured He'd grade on the curve, and I'd make it in easily.

I had surely tried to do things I thought God would give me credit for, but I still felt a little uneasy. I had high hopes, but I expected no advance notice of acceptance. You cannot imagine the relief I felt when I found out I could be sure I **The Teacher has taken the test for me, and He scored 100%!** had already been accepted because the Teacher has taken the test for me, and He scored 100%! I swallowed my pride and thanked Him.

A Divine Finale to the Feast of Tabernacles

The eighth day of the Feast of Tabernacles had prophetic overtones. On that day no water was poured on the altar. This was to celebrate the fact that when the Hebrew nation arrived in the Promised Land, God no longer had to supernaturally supply water from a rock. There are many references in the Old Testament linking water with the coming of the Messiah. They were celebrating by pouring water on the altar, and Jesus was there. The significance would not have been lost on any Jew who knew the Scriptures.

"On the last and greatest day of the Feast, Jesus stood and said in a loud voice, 'If anyone is thirsty, let him come to me and drink. Whoever believes in me, as the Scripture has said, streams of living water will flow from within him.'" (John 7:37-38) The offer to satisfy thirst—give satisfaction—was a claim to be the Messiah, to be God. His statement would have been recognized as a reference to Isaiah 55:1, "Come, all you who are thirsty, come to the waters..." In context, the passage in John is clearly a reference to the Messiah. Jesus had already told the woman at the well He was the living water. Now, He presented Himself in the Temple at the perfect moment to make that announcement to the assembled religious leaders of the nation. They were bound by their own presuppositions about their Messiah, unwilling to consider the validity of His claim, disturbed and frightened at the threat to the status quo. They intensified their efforts to arrest Him.

The throngs of pilgrims who heard the announcement remained divided in their opinion about Him. Some were open-minded and teachable; they were ready to make the most important decision they would ever make in their lives. However, many were so influenced by the negative leadership of the standard-bearers of the Jewish religion that they were paralyzed—unable to openly consider the possibility that Jesus was not a liar or a lunatic—but that *He was the Lord*, the Messiah they had long awaited.

For years I based my decisions about Jesus and the Bible on hearsay and half-truths. Then I realized the stupidity of making important choices without gathering the facts and weighing them carefully for myself. Have you come to that realization?

Father God,

I really want to be open-minded; I want to be teachable. I want to learn from Your Son, the Great Teacher. You have said if I am willing to do Your will, You will show me what is true. I need not only the ability to discern truth but also the ability to obey it. Please guide me and empower me. Amen.

Chapter 8

Attempted Entrapment

Chapter 8

Attempted Entrapment

The morning after the final ceremony of the Feast of Tabernacles Jesus was back in the Temple courtyard teaching. God the Father has carefully, sovereignly preserved in the Bible the record of His Son's words so that you can examine them firsthand. But don't just read the Bible to try to find a mistake. The teachers of the law and the Pharisees listened to Jesus with just such a motive. As lawyers they were undoubtedly trained to look for flaws in an argument, but exercising that skill to try to trap an adversary instead of to try to find the truth was wrong—and still is.

A Trap Is Set

The Pharisees had caught a woman in the act of adultery, and they thought they could exploit the situation to catch Jesus on the horns of a dilemma. They thought He'd have to say either to break the law of Moses or break the law of Rome. If He told them to carry out the law given by Moses and stone her, He would be arrested as an insurrectionist for only Rome had the authority to decree the death penalty for a citizen of a conquered nation. Moreover, if He told them to forgive her, He would be in trouble for not observing the religious law of His own nation which held she should be stoned to death. They thought they had Him. Jesus stooped down and started writing on the ground with His finger.

If Jesus were only a man, the uneducated son of a simple small-town carpenter, it is surprising that He knew how to write. Conversely, if Jesus were really God with the wisdom of the universe at His command, it is astonishing that this is the only record we have of His ever having written anything. If I were God and this illustrious young man were my only Son, I'm sure I'd have preserved His only written words; I would probably have had those words carved in stone, not scratched in dust. Wouldn't you love to know what He wrote? I would. However, God only promises to tell us what we need to know, not what we want to know to satisfy our curiosity. Actually, what He felt that day intrigues me more than what He wrote. He was confronted by an immoral woman and a group of religious leaders who were willing to sacrifice a woman to trap a man. They were powerful men bent on His destruction; yet, Jesus seemed to feel more compassion for the woman than He did concern for Himself.

Made in the Image of God

Paul Tournier in *The Meaning of Persons* says, "The minute people become things, the spirit of Christianity is dead." This woman was a "thing" to those men; they were using her. Jesus was the target of their hate, and she, who had perhaps once been the target of their lust, was now useful to them in another way. It is so wrong to use people and love things. Yet, Jesus saw each of those people that day as being made in the image of God. Distorted by hate, defiled by sexual immoralities, even those men and that woman still bore the hallmark of their Maker and were objects of His love. The spotlight of Jesus' steady, all-knowing gaze must have left the men feeling defenseless and the woman repentant. The woman's accusers left.

Jesus is compassionate and forgiving. He does not condemn us for unacceptable behavior nor does He condone our continuing in it. He exhorted the woman at the well, the man at the pool, and now the woman dragged out of an unholy bed. He urged each of them to abandon their former attitudes and actions in the light of His love for them. Jesus loves us enough to meet us where we are, but He loves us too much to leave us there.

Jesus does not condemn us for unacceptable behavior nor does He condone our continuing in it.

John 8:7-12

7 When they kept on questioning him, he straightened up and said to them, "If any one of you is without sin, let him be the first to throw a stone at her."

8 Again he stooped down and wrote on the ground.

9 At this, those who heard began to go away one at a time, the older ones first, until only Jesus was left, with the woman still standing there.

¹⁰ Jesus straightened up and asked her, "Woman, where are they? Has no one condemned you?"

¹¹ "No one, sir," she said. "Then neither do I condemn you," Jesus declared. "Go now and leave your life of sin."

¹² When Jesus spoke again to the people, he said, "I am the light of the world. Whoever follows me will never walk in darkness, but will have the light of life."

The Light of the World

The next time He spoke to a large crowd was to claim to be the Light of the World. Again the Pharisees recognized that Jesus was claiming to be co-equal with God. They challenged Him to produce a witness to verify His statement. He named His Father as the corroborating witness. Their resolve to be rid of Him intensified.

The determination of the religious leaders to reject the deity of Christ showed the decadence of their relationship with God. As their faith deteriorated, so did their world. The 1st century was a period in history when immorality, materialism and idolatry flourished. The same thing is true of the 21st century and for the same underlying cause. When religious leaders err in their belief and fail in their leadership, people of faith suffer, stumble and sometimes fall. The entire culture suffers decline.

> **When religious leaders err in their belief and fail in their leadership, people of faith suffer, stumble, and sometimes fall**

Are You Scared of the Dark?

I doubt if very many people believe the world is getting better. We have become a nation of ostriches in order to survive with a semblance of normalcy. Too much bad news has sent us scurrying for soft sand. Like little children afraid of the dark, we pull the covers over our heads. I personally have come to prefer the sports page to the front page of the morning paper. If my team wins, I feel good; if they lose, I can tell myself it doesn't really matter—it's only a game. Soft sand feels better than hard facts.

Several years ago I was participating in a retreat at a Christian conference center in the mountains. One night during a rainstorm, lightning hit a transformer and the whole camp was plunged into darkness. One of my sons had given me a tiny flashlight on a key chain. I told him it was cute and thanked him, but on the way back to the cabins its value increased exponentially. I made new friends instantly as I met their need for light. One woman gave up trying to stay close. The path seemed smooth, and she felt fairly secure until she tripped over a tree root that had pushed though the asphalt path. Down she went!

Many times I do not feel the need to stay close to the Light of the World when my life is going well. When the path is smooth, we all tend to get a little too self-confident. The most positive thing about spiritual darkness—the overwhelming problems in the world today—is that more people are becoming aware of their need to get near the Light.

No matter where you are—walking back to a cabin or traveling the world—a trip of any length requires light. Jesus said, "I am the light of the world." (John 8:12) Stay close so you won't stumble and fall.

Who Are God's Children?

The Jewish rulers would not accept the testimony of Jesus and His Father, although many of the people did. Jesus told the leaders if they truly followed Him they would know the truth and be liberated. Again they took His words so literally that they missed the point. They asserted they were not slaves and did not need to be set free. They were already God's children; they always had been. They were Jews, weren't they?

Do you think you are already a child of God because you were born in America, which at least used to be a Christian country or because you were born into a Christian family? Do you think you can have a relationship with God without faith in Jesus Christ? You should consider the response of Jesus carefully.

He told them that if they were really children of God they would love Him. The Father is totally unapproachable unless the Son takes you into His presence. There are a lot of important people in the world whom you will never get to meet unless someone you know knows them and introduces you. So, why do we balk at the suggestion that we can't know the Father unless His Son introduces us?

There are *not* many ways to God; there is only *one* way. The Jews did not become God's children automatically because of national or racial or familial descent. They were deceiving themselves. Jesus said to them, "You belong to your father, the **There are *not* many ways to God; there is only *one* way.** devil." (John 8:44) What an awful thing to say! But Jesus spoke the truth; He *is* the Truth; He cannot lie. We do take many different paths to arrive at the place where we recognize our need for God, then once we realize we need Him, He draws us to His Son and His Son brings us to His Father. Only the Son can take us to His Father. Until He does, we walk in darkness with the ruler of the kingdom of the air, the prince of darkness, as our guide. (Ephesians 2:2)

Children of Light, Children of Darkness

Jesus found another way of saying that the spiritual void we feel is actually a symptom of our spiritual deadness. We are born physically alive, but spiritually dead. We are not alive spiritually until we believe in Jesus as God's perfect provision for our need to walk in the Light. Until then we walk in the darkness and are actually children of Satan, guided by him.

Susan Atkins, a former member of the infamous Manson family, tells in her book, *Child of Satan, Child of God,* of being born into the family of God, experiencing forgiveness and of actually seeing in her prison mirror a clearly discernible change. She saw a light that came on in her once dull eyes. Perhaps because our sins have been less heinous and less publicized, our own birth into the family of God will not seem as dramatic nor get as much press coverage. However, Jesus told those religious leaders they needed to hear and believe God's truth in order to receive new life just as surely as that Judean prostitute did. Just as surely as Susan Atkins needed His cleansing power in her life, so did I and so do you.

Jesus, Our Judge

Few of us stray as far from the accepted behavioral norm of our society as that Jewish prostitute or Susan Atkins did. We carefully conceal our bad attitudes and wrong choices. King Solomon, perhaps the wisest man who ever lived, said in Proverbs 6:16,17—

"There are six things the LORD hates, seven that are detestable to him: haughty eyes, a lying tongue, hands that shed innocent blood, a heart that devises wicked schemes, feet that are quick to rush into evil, a false witness who pours out lies and a man who stirs up dissension among brothers." Surprisingly, a "proud look" (from the King James Version of the Bible) or, "haughty eyes" (from the NIV)—a covert attitude is listed before the overt act of murder in the list of things God hates. God does not always see things the same way we do; He will not judge by our standards.

Today tolerance is ranked above holiness as a virtue in most people's minds. When my son Rick was attending the University of Southern California, he came home one day and said, "Mom, they want us to be so open-minded our brains will fall out." As a nation and as individuals, I think there is evidence that our brains have fallen out. We tolerate behavior that violates God's law set forth in His Book, and we harbor attitudes that God hates—but not with impunity! God the Father has committed to His Son the job of judging the whole world. He will make no mistakes.

Today tolerance is ranked above holiness as a virtue in most people's minds.

Dear God,

Our world is getting so dark that it sometimes frightens me. I find myself wishing I could hold Your hand as if I were a little girl afraid of the dark. However, let me retain a healthy fear of darkness and confront it—not to conquer the fear but to conquer the darkness. Please guide me along the path of life so I can clearly see the difference between right and wrong. Please, God, don't let me get so messed up in my thinking that I use people and love things. Teach me to let Your Word judge me instead of me thinking I have the right or the wisdom to judge Your Word. Our world is getting darker; don't let me stumble in the dark. Let me instead shed light in our sin-sick world. Amen.

Chapter 9

Man in the Dark

Chapter 9

Man in the Dark

Jesus can relate to losers. This is an almost unbelievable statement, but I believe it to be true. Why?—because the Bible tells us He loves the whole world, and this world includes a lot of losers! Jesus, who came to show us what the Father is like, loved them and helped them. We should not do less.

The life of Jesus is a pattern for our lives. He is a great deal more than a man to be copied, but that doesn't mean that His life is not to be emulated. Our first "good work" is to believe in Him as being the One especially sent by the Father. Having laid that foundation we should build on it. Having done that good work of believing, we should do other good things as a result of our faith, our gratitude and our love for the One who died for us and showed us how to live.

A Balance of Faith and Works

Over the last several decades there has been a real split in the professing Christian church between those who advocate getting involved in trying to solve the social problems of our world and those who think the job of the church is simply to preach the gospel. Jesus divides people all right, but this is a senseless division. Christians who promote a social gospel often show concern only for the physical, material and temporal needs of the ones to whom they minister; they often neglect their spiritual needs. The pure gospel advocates—the evangelicals—believe the prime function of the church is to tell people the good news of Jesus' death and resurrection so they can be rightly related to God; they often ignore the practical needs of the ones they seek to save. Both are right—but only half right. Jesus exhorted people to be right with God the Father through faith in Him and thus be eternally safe, but He was also concerned for their temporal needs. If He were living today, He might confuse as many people as He did in the 1st century. Some would label Him a "do-gooder;" He sure did a lot of good and was concerned for peoples' temporal, material needs. He also repeatedly told people they had to believe in Him. He constantly, consistently preached the truth about the way to be saved. He kept His balance perfectly—never leaning too far in one direction or the other. If you pay careful attention to His words and His actions, it is obvious Jesus is not an either/or person but rather that He is a both/and person.

Increasing publicity regarding welfare frauds and growing concern over the crushing tax load has created a hazard for us who try to keep our balance between these two facets of faith. There is a temptation to overreact, to be blinded to legitimate needs and to be unfeeling toward persons less fortunate than we are. It's a lot less costly just to tell hungry, homeless people of their need to believe in Jesus than it is to actually try to feed and house them.

God's Welfare Plan

The greatest kind of welfare in the world is personal concern for and involvement with an individual in need. As Jesus came out of the Temple one day, God placed such a man right in His path. He perceived that helping this man was one of His assigned chores.

I love the continuity, the flow of Scripture. Jesus had told everyone within shouting distance that He was the Light of the World. Now, He reasserted this claim to the blind man immediately before miraculously giving him his sight. The physical blindness of this man is a graphic picture of the spiritual blindness which affects so many. Although Jesus can still heal both kinds of blindness, today His emphasis is on healing spiritual blindness.

> The physical blindness of this man is a graphic picture of the spiritual blindness which affects so many.

A Little More Light

There is a principle that runs through the whole Bible: you must be obedient to act upon the revelation, the enlightenment God gives you, before He will give you more. There is no better illustration of this principle than this story of the blind man.

I experienced the principle played out in my own life. Having trusted Christ as my Savior as a child, as a young adult my intellectual pride and "busyness" very effectively shut down my pursuit of

God. He let me go my own way for years. If I was content to ignore what I knew, He was content to ignore me it seemed. Truth not applied is truth denied. Truth denied and not applied stops the flow of revelation. As I've already mentioned,

Truth not applied is truth denied.

God finally had to knock me down on a ski slope in Sun Valley to get my attention. I now know He was there in the background—waiting—for all those years before He finally became pro-active. How grateful I am that He cared enough to finally take action.

John 9:1-5

1   As he went along, he saw a man blind from birth.
2   His disciples asked him, "Rabbi, who sinned, this man or his parents, that he was born blind?"
3   "Neither this man nor his parents sinned," said Jesus, "but this happened so that the work of God might be displayed in his life.
4   As long as it is day, we must do the work of him who sent me. Night is coming, when no one can work.
5   While I am in the world, I am the light of the world."

Jesus made a mud paste and put it on the blind man's eyes and told him to go wash it off in the pool of Siloam. The man obeyed and his sight was restored. At that time the superstitious belief was that the spittle of a fasting man had curative power. Some modern theologians in their efforts to explain away Jesus' miracles have assumed Jesus was fasting and, thus, the mud made with His spittle restored the man's sight. Sometimes, we discard the miraculous that is supra-reason to embrace that which is contra-reason.

God can use current medical knowledge to heal, and my own belief is that there is nothing unspiritual about taking advantage of new medical discoveries and skills as long as we remember that all healing ultimately comes from God. He can heal through a doctor or a new "wonder drug," or He can heal with a touch.

Who Made You See?

The blind man was healed when he acted in faithful obedience to Jesus whom he knew only as "a man they call Jesus." (John 9:11)

Just as they had with the man by the pool of Bethesda, the Pharisees angrily accused Jesus of being ungodly because He had healed this man on the Sabbath. Even though he also faced ridicule, the man then declared that the One who healed him must be a prophet.

Then the Jews asked the man's parents how their son was healed. "Ask him," they replied. For the 1st century Jew, social as well as religious life revolved around the synagogue. The leaders had decided to excommunicate anyone who believed that Jesus was the Messiah. As a result of that decision, the blind man's parents made their decision that they were not willing to get involved with Jesus. Though the man knew his own parents would not risk excommunication to stand with him, he bravely ventured into a little theological discussion with the religious experts of his day. That took courage! There was a lot he didn't know, but like the woman at the well, he opted for taking a stand and talking about what he *did* know.

God Seeks Man

The Jewish rulers threw the blind man out of the Temple because he would not deny what had happened to him. Jesus went looking for him not only to comfort him, but also, I am convinced, to teach him. He wants us to be able to give intelligent reasons for our beliefs. He doesn't want our faith based *solely* on personal experience because that won't necessarily stand up when the memory or the emotion fades. So, the Teacher sought him out to teach him. A well-balanced, enduring faith includes both knowledge and personal experience, our head and heart—intelligence and emotion—both involved. We must not be either/or people as far as faith and works are concerned or as far as knowledge and experience are concerned. Jesus was a both/and person; He is an excellent role model.

I love the fact that Jesus goes looking for people—like Philip and the man born blind. God the Father sought out Adam and Eve when they were separated from Him in the Garden of Eden by their own deliberate disobedience. They hid from God, but He went looking for them. Even if our separation from God is self-induced, God still goes looking for us.

Jesus went looking for the man born blind. He sought him, found him and helped him grow to the point that he worshipped Him as Lord.

Stages of Development

Research into an infant's physical development points to the importance of crawling before walking. Lance, the youngest of our four children was so eager to keep up with the "thundering herd" of his siblings that the minute he was put in a stroller he managed to kick away the footrest and convert it into a walker—and walk he did—or actually, run he did. Because he had mobility before he had any judgment at all, he managed to run his machine off the edge of the pool at his grandparents' house and was still trying to drive it up the other side when his big sister dove in and rescued him. He seemed determined not to go through the necessary stages of development.

The world recognizes that we go through psychological, emotional and physical stages of development. Why do we expect instant maturity in the spiritual realm? Perhaps it's because we have grown accustomed to instant everything from instant coffee to instant mashed potatoes. And God forbid that we should have to wait 30 seconds for our computers to come on! Instant gratification is the rule of the day.

But maturing in our faith is a process. Few people blossom overnight into spiritual giants of the faith. "The man they call Jesus," "a prophet," "a man from God," "the Son of Man worthy of worship"—step by step the man born blind responded to the spiritual light that he was given and grew in his understanding of who Jesus is. If we move too fast we risk making mistakes in judgment.

Study the Cast of Characters

There are some interesting characters in this story. There were the religious people with the mindset that Jesus was not God. Their minds were made up; they would not consider the evidence. Then there were the parents of the man born blind who were unwilling to become identified with Jesus because of the social and religious ostracism they knew would follow. And finally, there was the man born blind. Realizing he was helpless to solve his own problem, responding in faith to enlightenment as he received it, receiving healing and finally offering worship to "the man they call Jesus," he was changed. He was so changed that people who had known him since he was a child couldn't believe he was the same person. With which of these people do you identify?

Dear God,

I want to be like the blind man—so changed I am unrecognizable to old friends. I realize that I have considerable information now and that I will not receive more until I have responded in faith to what I already have. I guess I wanted to understand everything before I acted on anything. I realize now that I can't come head first into the Kingdom of God. There is still a lot I don't understand, but I do want to grow. Give me the courage to take a stand on what I do know and the patience to go through the process of maturing into a Christian with a growing knowledge of who You are, who Jesus is and what You expect of me. Amen.

Interlude

When I returned to Texas for my 40th high school reunion celebration, I had been teaching the Bible for almost 20 years. During my high school years I was always up for a party. I was a fun-loving, jitterbugging teenager. At the reunion several people who heard I was now a "Bible teacher" expressed surprise at the change in me. I was both pleased and perplexed that they saw such a difference. I still loved to dance; I still loved a party; but apparently I was different in some way that was obvious to them. I felt like I was the "same old me," but evidently I wasn't. Jesus does change us—and it is always for the better—for which I am very grateful.

Chapter 10

Sheep in the Pasture

Chapter 10

Sheep in the Pasture

John 10 is one of my favorite chapters in the Bible. I think I love it so much because I loved my father so much. Jesus had just revealed Himself to and received worship from the healed blind man. Now, He turns His attention to the leaders of the Jews who were overly preoccupied with keeping the letter of their interpretation of the law. As they struggled to preserve the status quo, Jesus continued to communicate God's truth. He used a figure of speech that should have been readily understandable to anyone who lived in that rural environment. Jesus said He was the Good Shepherd.

John 10:14, 15

14 "I am the good shepherd; I know my sheep and my sheep know me—

15 just as the Father knows me and I know the Father—and I lay down my life for the sheep."

My Father Was a Rancher

A beautiful creek meandered through the ranch where I grew up. Daddy ran cattle across the creek, but over by the house he had a flock of sheep. He was a good shepherd. He knew and loved all his animals, and they knew and loved him. When I was a little girl, I often went to the pasture with him.

Daddy had a different call for the sheep, goats, cows, and even the pigs. He could call everyone of his animals right up to him. Years later when I went home for visits, Daddy drove his pick-up truck to the pasture across the creek. His voice wasn't as strong as it once was, but the cows had learned to recognize the sound of the horn on his truck. He'd drive up and honk, and they'd come from over the hill or out of a thicket of brush and trees. Any other horn?—they'd scatter in the opposite direction. The sheep in the pasture in back of the house still got to hear his voice.

Why Sheep?

I used to wonder when I first started reading the Bible before I got a clear picture of God—and myself—why God would compare us to sheep. There is nothing more appealing than a little fluffy white lamb, but a grown sheep is a dirty gray, runny-nosed, smelly, downright unappealing animal. It's certainly not very flattering to think God sees us as that far from being perfect, but the good news is that He still loves us.

I'll never forget standing on the steps of the back porch one afternoon watching a flock of sheep walk across the pasture single file. A bee stung the old ewe at the head of the line making her jump. Every single sheep in that line jumped right at the same spot even though she had no reason to do so. Sheep play follow the leader to the point of absurdity. Thoughtless conformity is their life style.

No wonder God calls us sheep. We are such followers of the latest trend, such pushovers to peer pressure, such unthinking conformists. If it's "in" to say there are mistakes in the Bible and it cannot be taken literally, we go right along with the crowd—at least I did for years. I was so concerned about what other people thought that I wasn't really thinking for myself.

I was so concerned about what other people thought that I wasn't really thinking for myself.

I heard of a well-controlled experiment in which several people were shown a sheet of paper with varying lengths of lines drawn on it and were asked to identify the longest line. Every person but one was secretly told to select a specific line which was obviously not the longest. The one who was uninformed consistently changed his decision to stand with the others, though he knew they were wrong. Interestingly, if only one of the control group gave the correct answer, the incognizant one would stick with the right answer but would almost never "fly solo."

It's hard to stand alone, but God can give you the courage to do it and the strength to succeed. That tendency toward mass conformity is undoubtedly one reason Jesus refers to us as sheep.

Sheep Need a Shepherd

Remember Jesus' desire to provide food for Galilean picnickers? The prime responsibility of a shepherd is to make sure his sheep are well fed, and a good shepherd is concerned for the quality of the food his flock eats. I'm so glad I have a Shepherd who cares about what I eat. Honestly, one of my favorite meals is a hamburger, French fries and a chocolate milk shake, but my God-guided conscience won't let me indulge too often. I also enjoy reading the latest novel on the Top Ten list. When I was a freshman in college, my professor of English literature told me if I wanted to have a comic book mind I should read comic books, but he recommended Shakespeare. He was a good professor. Jesus is a Good Shepherd. He's concerned about what we feed our bodies—and our minds—in order to stay healthy.

A shepherd also provides shelter for his flock. My Daddy could always pen the sheep easily if they were hungry. All he had to do was shake a tin bucket full of dry corn, and they would all come running—with the exception of one old ewe who would just stare at him and walk away. "She'll have to get hungry enough to swallow her pride, or she'll **God wants to protect us— not from roaming coyotes, but from following wrong thinking friends.** be alone when she faces the danger I'm trying to protect her from. She's such a stubborn, proud old girl," he said. God wants to protect us—not from roaming coyotes, but from following wrong-thinking friends. But, like sheep, we have to choose to be protected. Sheep can't be driven like cattle because they scatter. To herd sheep is almost as impossible as herding cats. Sheep have to be led.

Daddy would entice the sheep to follow him into the pen by shaking that can. He'd leave the gate open just a crack so the sheep had to enter single file. He'd stand there and check each one as they came through. They all looked alike to me—but not to Daddy. He knew each one of them. He even had them named, usually by some distinguishing physical characteristic. But their name wasn't all he knew; he knew *everything* about them. One old ewe limped, and he checked her leg; another was prone to infection, and he looked her over carefully; another had lost her baby, and he stroked her ears and spoke reassuringly to her. He really cared, and they sensed it. My Daddy showed me what a good shepherd is like. Jesus is that Good Shepherd who cares about us the same way my father cared about his sheep.

The Picture of a Shepherd

One of the finest collections of art in the world is in the museum at the Vatican. You can walk and look for hours and not see everything, and after a while, you can't remember anything you've seen. But one beautiful little sculpture I will never forget. About 12 to 18 inches high and made of solid gold, it portrays Jesus as the Good Shepherd. Several sheep surround Him, and He is carrying a little lamb over His shoulders.

One spring when Daddy was almost 80, I went home without husband or children just to spend a few days with my parents. Mother had called to say the bluebonnets were so prolific and so beautiful on the ranch because it had been a hard winter. Strange that harsh conditions have a tendency to bring out the best in wild flowers—as well as people. The promise of fields of bluebonnets will get me on a plane to Texas quicker than almost anything; so there I was. I arrived on a beautiful balmy day; the bluebonnets were an especially deep blue, and they were so abundant that their fragrance filled the air. A special bonus was that the ewes were already lambing; so I got to see baby lambs—so appealing.

They say if you don't like the weather in Texas, wait ten minutes. Sure enough—running true to form—that night there was a blue norther—a late freeze—leaving the ground and high grass in the pastures covered with frost. I heard Daddy get up early to go check on the sheep. I dressed quickly and joined him. His concern was for the safety of any lamb that might have been born during the night.

By the early dawn light, visibility was poor so Daddy and I walked a pattern through the tall, frost-covered grass looking for new babies. Daddy found one! Already chilled to the bone, not even able to walk, that little lamb had found sanctuary in Daddy's arms—cuddled against his chest inside his unzipped jacket. My Dad approached me from across the pasture just as the sun came up. The tender look on his face told me of his concern for the little lamb he was carrying to safety. My mind went back to that statue in the Vatican, which reminded me of a passage in the Old Testament book of Isaiah.

Our Shepherd Cares for Us

It's actually hard to fathom that the Creator of the universe has the time or inclination to be personally involved with each of His created creatures. However, the Bible says He does. Isaiah 40:11 reads, "He tends his flock like a shepherd: He gathers the lambs in his arms and carries them close to his heart; he gently leads those that have young." In verse 12, there is a rather abrupt change; it says: "Who has measured the waters in the hollow of his hand, or with the breadth of his hand marked off the heavens? Who has held the dust of the earth in a basket, or weighed the mountains on the scales and the hills in a balance?"

There is balanced teaching in the Bible which states that God is the great creative force who spoke everything into existence *and* that He is a personal God who cares for each one of us individually. Amazing! God knows your name; He knows my name. He created us—and the world in which we live—and yet He is a personal God who cares for each of us individually—and tenderly. He protects us; He feeds us; He leads us.

Our Shepherd Leads Us

There are many ways God leads. The Pharisees thought they had put the man born blind out of the synagogue. Actually, God had used them to bring him out. God's friends are His co-workers; His enemies are His tools. Because He is a sovereign God in control of the universe He created, He can lead through circumstances, and He can lead **God's friends are His co-workers; His enemies are His tools.** through people—even people who don't believe He exists. He also can and does just give quiet, inner assurance of the way we are supposed to go and the things we are supposed to do. Dr. J. Sidlow Baxter posed the question in the title of one of his books, *Does God Still Guide?* Everything in that book points to the fact that the answer is a resounding *yes!*

Jesus, the True Shepherd

Jesus is the true Shepherd. He used this analogy several times. First, He declared Himself to be the Shepherd who entered the sheepfold by the appointed way, doubtless referring to His credentials as the long-awaited Messiah. Proof of His claim included His fulfillment of many Old Testament prophecies. Jesus was born at the right time in the right town of the right tribe; He was a legitimate heir to the throne of King David. He was no false shepherd who would put a sheep out of the sheepfold as the rabbis had done to the blind man.

Jesus spoke very clearly, yet the Jews did not understand Him. Unlike some modern theologians, He never confused his audience by using a lot of big words with obscure meanings. Someone counted His words which are quoted in the New Testament; He used approximately 200 words. (Many editions of the Bible print the words Jesus spoke in red to emphasize their importance.) Surely, He limited the number of words He used only because of His desire to speak simply, concisely and understandably. I'm sure He had an unlimited vocabulary; He had the wisdom of the ages at His command.

Jesus never confused his audience by using a lot of big words with obscure meanings.

Jesus, the Gate

After saying He was the Shepherd who entered the sheepfold the proper way, He changed the metaphor and said He was the only way into the sheepfold. This picture is clearly that of a Bedouin shepherd, not a Texas rancher. In the Middle East during the summer sheep were allowed to graze in pastures enclosed by rock walls with openings to other pastures. At night the shepherd penned the sheep in one enclosed pasture and lay down across the opening which meant his body literally became the gate. No malicious person or marauding animal could get to the sheep to steal them or harm them without stepping over the shepherd. A good shepherd would fight to the death to protect his sheep. Jesus said He would lay down His life for His sheep.

He did just that so we might have eternal life and be rightly related to God forever. There is only one way into that relationship—one gate into that eternal sheepfold. Jesus is that one way.

John 10:7-9

7 Therefore Jesus said again, "I tell you the truth, I am the gate for the sheep.

8 All who ever came before me were thieves and robbers, but the sheep did not listen to them.

9 I am the gate; whoever enters through me will be saved. He will come in and go out, and find pasture."

In the pasture there is promised abundance, not necessarily of material things, but of satisfying experiences. The grass may be greener on the other side of the fence—the world does entice—but it is certainly safer to graze close to the Shepherd.

Safely in the Fold

Once in the fold you'll never want to leave and no one can force you out. The Shepherd assumes the responsibility for keeping you safely in the fold. Jesus said:

John 10:28-30

28 "I give them eternal life, and they shall never perish; no one can snatch them out of my hand.

29 My Father, who has given them to me, is greater than all; no one can snatch them out of my Father's hand.

30 I and the Father are one."

One of the most revolutionary aspects of this promised security is not an addition, but a subtraction—the Lord takes away your fear of death. Knowing that could revolutionize your life. There are increasing numbers of hospices that are especially equipped to alleviate the physical and emotional pain of dying. However, the greatest ministry to a dying person is to eliminate the *fear* of death. Knowing the Good Shepherd can do that.

Jesus' offer of eternal life left the people divided again. Many of the Jews were still undecided. They had heard His amazing words; they had seen His miraculous works. But they had expected the Messiah to be a political deliverer who would lead them to freedom from Rome. Therefore, their leaders did not accept Him. They challenged Him to tell them plainly if He were the Messiah. Jesus answered, "I did tell you but you do not believe." (John 10:25) He had no intention of giving them any more light until they acted on the light they had. They steadfastly refused to do that. Instead, without excuse for not understanding that He claimed to be equal with God the Father and apparently determined not to believe that He actually was, they willfully made the decision to stone Him to death for blasphemy. Jesus left them and went back across the Jordan River to tend to His sheep who were waiting there.

Are You Hungry?

My Daddy used to do that too. He'd just leave and go across the creek to see about the other stock when the sheep would not follow him into the pen. He didn't try to force his care on them; he preferred to just come back later. Daddy said the biggest problem he had penning the sheep was when the grazing was so good outside in the pasture that they felt no hunger for the grain he offered. Also, when weather conditions were mild, they sensed no need for the protection of the pen.

Are you satisfied with what the world has to offer—satisfied with its pleasure, unthreatened by its danger? Are you hungry enough to swallow your pride and admit you need a Savior? If you are still in complete control of your own life, maybe you don't feel the need to follow anyone else. But remember, the Shepherd is waiting to help, protect, lead and feed. If you're not ready, He'll come back later....

Dear God,
Maybe I'd better follow Jesus now. Something might happen to me before the Good Shepherd gets back. Amen.

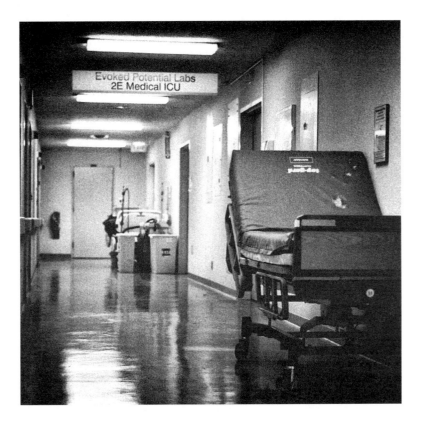

Chapter 11

A Tale of Two Sisters

Chapter 11

A Tale of Two Sisters

Concerned for His own physical life and the spiritual life of the people across the Jordan River, Jesus returned there and stayed until His friends Mary and Martha sent for Him. When He received the message that their brother was critically ill, He delayed going to them for two days. Then, in spite of the personal danger of going so near Jerusalem, He went to their home in Bethany. He had been there many times before. When He was in Jerusalem it was an easy walk to their house, and there He was always sure of a warm welcome, a good bed and some of Martha's cooking.

John 11:1-4

1 Now a man named Lazarus was sick. He was from Bethany, the village of Mary and her sister Martha.

2 This Mary, whose brother Lazarus now lay sick, was the same one who poured perfume on the Lord and wiped his feet with her hair.

3 So the sisters sent word to Jesus, "Lord, the one you love is sick."

4 When he heard this, Jesus said, "This sickness will not end in death. No, it is for God's glory so that God's Son may be glorified through it."

One Man's Family

Theirs was an interesting, unusual family. Little is known of Lazarus, except that he was the brother of Martha and Mary and was a close friend of Jesus. Martha was obviously the family leader, a worker who accepted responsibility, apparently without hesitation, but not always without complaint. The text implies she was a compulsive housekeeper and cook. She seemed unable to relax and do things casually and easily, and she was prone to self-pity when her sister didn't help her do things the hard way. She must have practically "lived in the kitchen." She was prepared, purposeful, and perhaps a little "prissy." Mary, on the other hand, was patient, pensive and I always think of her as more than a little pretty. Her nature would desire "fig tree time." When Jesus was there, she sat on the floor at His feet and soaked up every word He said. These two sisters were certainly different, but they both loved Jesus.

Take a Good Look at Jesus

Where did the picture of Jesus as a physical weakling originate? It was certainly not from the Biblical accounts. In art, He is usually portrayed as slim to the point of being emaciated and somewhat effeminate in spite of the fact that He lived and slept outdoors, repeatedly traversed the nation of Israel on foot, and formerly supported himself as a carpenter—and before the electric saw! The Man may not have been a hunk, but He undoubtedly had muscles.

Where did the picture of Jesus as an emotional weakling originate? Was it in His own statement that He was "meek and lowly?" (Matthew 11:29) What a perversion of the meaning of those words. As a man He consistently evidenced great strength of character, walking into mortal danger with a fair degree of regularity without a hint of either cowardice or exaggerated "macho-type" bravado. Jesus was clearly in control and yet was simultaneously in submission to His Father's will. He was a busy man, successfully involved in His Father's business; yet, He was involved with people. He found time to cultivate deep friendships with at least twelve men and certainly with Lazarus and his sisters.

Jesus was clearly in control and was yet simultaneously in submission to His Father's will.

Jesus' fine sense of timing never failed Him. However, when He heard about his friend's illness, He waited two days before returning to the Jerusalem area. Because of Bethany's proximity to Jerusalem, home of the Jewish leaders who were Jesus' avowed enemies, the disciples feared for His life—and theirs—if they accompanied Him on this trip. It was dangerous for Jesus to go to His friends, but only a false shepherd would flee when the sheep need help.

Why, God?

When Jesus arrived, Lazarus was already dead. Martha rushed out to meet Him, ready to complain about His delayed arrival. "If you had been here, my brother would not have died," she said. (John 11:21)

I have said, "If you had answered when I prayed the first time, this would not have happened." What suppressed animosity toward God we feel because He didn't heal our loved one, answer our prayer, or solve our problem when or how we thought He should. We naturally assume that if He loved us, He wouldn't let this happen. Thus, we allow ourselves to feel unloved by Him or unloving toward Him. Yet, the text says, "Jesus loved Martha and her sister and Lazarus." (John 11:5), and it states that there was benefit for the disciples and glory for God the Father and His Son in this apparent tragedy.

It's hard to see how believers can be helped and God can be glorified by some of the pain and suffering in the world. Frankly, I am looking forward with keen anticipation to an explanation when I get to Heaven. In the meantime, I have chosen to believe that His word is truth; His character is loving; His timing is perfect. Sometimes that's not easy!

Jesus Confronts Martha

C. S. Lewis in his book *The Problem of Pain* says, "God whispers to us in our pleasures, speaks to us in our conscience, but shouts to us in our pain." One of the good things that came out of this untimely death was that Jesus got Martha out of the kitchen long enough to talk to her. I'm one of those now fairly rare women who still love to cook and take the time to do it, but I notice that a trial or tragedy can get me to put my cookbook down and pick up my Bible quicker than anything else.

> "God whispers to us in our pleasures, speaks to us in our conscience, but shouts to us in our pain."

Now that Jesus had Martha's attention, He started to teach her. She had a somewhat nebulous belief in the resurrection from the dead. She knew Jesus could have saved her brother's life if He had chosen to, but she did not believe Jesus was co-equal with God. In other words, she did not believe, at this point, that He was the

Christ, the Messiah. She said she knew God would give Him whatever He asked, but in the original Greek the verb translated "ask" is the one used of a slave asking a favor of his master. To this highly intelligent woman with so many questions, Jesus chose to reveal His deity by telling her, "I am the resurrection and the life. He who believes in me will live, even though he dies; and whoever lives and believes in me will never die." (John 11:25) And she believed; she saw the Light; she knew He was the Christ, the unique Son of God, the Messiah.

It's good to get out of the kitchen and spend a little time at the feet of the Master. Her faith grew when she did—so does mine when I do—so will yours if you will. Maybe it's not a cookbook you need to put down—maybe it's a tennis racquet or a golf club or a deck of cards or the latest novel or your cell phone or your laptop or your Blackberry. Maybe you need just to have some time to think. If you still have small children, get a sitter. If you have a job, take an afternoon off. Whatever it is that distracts you and keeps you from taking the time to figure out who Jesus really is—that thing is your enemy!

> **Whatever it is that distracts you and keeps you from taking the time to figure out who Jesus really is—that thing is your enemy!**

Jesus Comforts Mary

Though Martha had rushed out to meet Jesus, Mary waited quietly until He sent for her. She came to Jesus with her heartbreak, weeping openly. Jesus' response to Martha was to teach her; His response to Mary was to cry with her. How different we are! How different our needs! How different His response to us!

I am fascinated with this story of these two sisters because of the study in personalities it affords. Martha was naturally a doer; Mary was a thinker. Martha was eager, aggressive and independent. She was so capable, so organized that she must have been tempted to plan her life without Jesus and then just fit Him in around the edges. He was not central in her life or her thinking. Mary was sensitive, retiring, and more dependent. She had no tendency to organize Jesus out of her life, but she did tend to get depressed over the problems that He allowed her to experience.

Quenchers and Grievers

The Bible exhorts us in 1 Thessalonians 5:19 to "quench not the Spirit" and in Ephesians 4:30 to "grieve not the Holy Spirit of God." Our personality determines which we are more prone to do. Some of us are so afraid to trust God that we hang back analyzing ourselves, our motives, our inabilities until we experience an overwhelming sense of inadequacy that leads to paralysis by analysis. Thus we have effectively put out the Spirit's fire. Some of us rush out ahead of the Lord, grieving Him as we act with the insensitivity of the proverbial "bull in a china closet." There are "quenchers" and "grievers." It appears to me Mary was a quencher and Martha was a griever.

There are many different psychological inventories used to determine your basic personality traits. Before Tim LaHaye co-wrote the best selling series, *Left Behind,* he wrote and spoke about personality types. I remember hearing him say that he could discern your basic type in 10 minutes unless you had been "walking with the Lord" for awhile. If you had, he said it became much harder because God Himself changed you; He strengthened your weaknesses and brought your strengths under control. I am convinced God does do that. Therefore, "quenchers" are not so fearful and reticent about stepping out and "grievers" are not so bold and quick to rush out. Wouldn't you love to have God Himself working to mold you into the person He created you to be? Do you know what your natural tendency is? I'm a quencher—a recovering quencher!

Lazarus Returns from the Dead

When Jesus went out to the tomb of Lazarus with the two sisters He was deeply grieved, even though He knew that in a matter of moments He was going to call Lazarus out of that grave—call him by name. One day we will all come out of the grave at the sound of His voice, but on this particular day, He only wanted Lazarus. Perhaps if He hadn't called Lazarus by name all the graves in that cemetery would have emptied! Jesus stood in a place where He was visible to all, and in broad daylight called to Lazarus in a loud, clear voice. To the astonishment of all watching, Lazarus did indeed come forth, grave clothes and all. He was physically restored to life. What took place in Bethany was very different from the murmured incantations usually muttered in a darkened room late at night as necromancers try to contact the dead.

Life after Death

Dr. Elizabeth Kubler-Ross and Dr. Raymond Moody have both done considerable research and extensive writing on the phenomenon of a person coming back from the dead. For the record, Lazarus had been dead four days. In King James English, Martha told the Lord of Life that Lazarus "stinketh." In other words, his body had started to decay. Yet Jesus restored him to life.

This was not a phenomenon similar to what Dr. Moody discusses in *Life After Death*—this was a miracle. I do, however, find his book fascinating, though I've known for a long time that there is "life after life." No doubt, people who find it easier to believe men than God have had their thinking influenced by his book.

Incidentally, God in *His* book gives us important information that Dr. Moody does not make clear. There is not only "life after life," but there is also "death after death." The soul and spirit of man live forever—only the body dies. After physical death, no matter what the cause, our spirits will either continue to experience eternal life or eternal death. Death in both the physical and spiritual sense involves separation. When an unbeliever's body dies, his soul and spirit will experience eternal separation from God. When a believer's body dies, eternal life—which begins when you are born into God's family—continues.

Jesus calls us to life—eternal life—and He calls us by name.

Jesus calls us to life...and He calls us by name. Have you ever heard Him call your name? Have you ever heard Him say, "Susie, come forth;" "Laura, come forth;" "Janice, come forth;" "Emily, come forth." Have you answered His call and stepped from death into life—eternal life?

Lord,

I have a lot to learn about You and a lot to learn about myself. I'm not even sure if I'm a Mary or a Martha—a quencher or a griever—but I'm trying to learn about me—and You. I definitely want to experience life after life, not death after death. Show me what I need to read or who I need to talk to in order to continue to grow in spiritual maturity. Amen.

Chapter 12

A Celebration of Life

Chapter 12

A Celebration of Life

When Jesus restored life to a man who had been dead four days, it created quite a stir. There were many witnesses, and they lost no time spreading the word. The chief priests and the Pharisees realized the situation was getting out of hand and issued a warrant for Jesus' arrest. They had predetermined He was to receive the death penalty. Jesus immediately withdrew into the desert with His disciples, but He returned to Bethany to attend a party given in His honor.

John 12:1-3

1   Six days before the Passover, Jesus arrived at Bethany, where Lazarus lived, whom Jesus had raised from the dead.

2   Here a dinner was given in Jesus' honor. Martha served, while Lazarus was among those reclining at the table with him.

3   Then Mary took about a pint of pure nard, an expensive perfume; she poured it on Jesus' feet and wiped his feet with her hair. And the house was filled with the fragrance of the perfume.

A Celebration Is in Order

A man named Simon, whom Jesus had healed of leprosy, was the host of the dinner party. Lazarus was a guest, and Mary and Martha were both there to help.

Let's look at these two sisters again. In Chapter 10 of Luke's gospel, Martha was preparing dinner for four—just the three members of her own family plus Jesus. She was uptight, not handling an unexpected guest easily and criticizing Mary for not helping. In John 11 she was complaining to Jesus about not meeting her time schedule, not solving her problem her way. Then, Jesus revealed to her who He really was—and she believed.

It appears to me that Martha may have been a bit obsessive-compulsive. Do you tend to plan your life so carefully and be so organized that it would "throw" you if something unplanned happened? Think about the difference it made in Martha's ability to "roll with the punches" when she relinquished the control of her life to Jesus.

A Change of Venue

I think one of the things that causes people to defer a decision about Jesus is the fear that He may try to make some enormous—to them catastrophic—change in their plans. Though most of us are very protective of our own game plans, He knows the Master Plan. My husband had a disgruntled friend during World War II. Equipped with a Ph.D. in psychology, he was not assigned to a position in personnel but was used as a typist for the Quartermaster Corps. That was definitely a waste of his training.

On the other hand, Jesus is not likely to squander your training and talent. If you are good in the kitchen and like to be there, you'll very likely still be there. Martha was, but with a difference. The Lord didn't ask her to go to Africa as a missionary, but she did end up doing something almost as disconcerting—going into someone else's kitchen to prepare and serve a large dinner party.

Jesus was there plus his twelve disciples along with Lazarus and Simon, but Martha was calm and in control. She was still in her own home town doing what she did best but with a changed attitude. She wasn't even mad at Mary for not helping. And what of Mary—what was she doing? She was still sitting at Jesus' feet, but she too had been changed.

Inappropriate Emotions or Appropriate Worship?

Of all the people at the party, Mary alone comprehended what Jesus had been telling them about His impending death. She was still the quiet one; so I'm sure her public display of honor and love was difficult. However, her understanding forced her action. Letting her hair down in public was definitely not her style, but her love for Jesus emboldened her. With tears of gratitude for what He had already done for her and tears of grief for what she understood He was about to do for her, she anointed Jesus' feet with oil and dried them with her hair. The men criticized her as a silly, emotional woman—she had deliberately risked that.

I have a friend who had been a life-long church member. A growing friendship between her family and ours challenged her to re-examine her faith. After some soul searching, some book reading and some thoughtful conversations, she made a brand new commitment to Christ. It was an exciting experience for her. She was not overly emotional, but her emotions were certainly involved. With some trepidation, she decided to tell her husband what had happened. His response was to say, "You'll get over it; such emotionalism won't last; and besides, it's unhealthy." Telling him was a risk she deliberately took, and she suffered the embarrassment of being labeled a silly, emotional woman. Her pride was hurt, but her faith was strengthened. She continued to be involved with Jesus at every level: physically she served Him; intellectually she studied and learned more of Him; emotionally she experienced His love. Eventually, her husband acknowledged the validity of her experience because it lasted and because it changed her.

That's how it should be. That kind of total commitment must be satisfying, not just to the one experiencing it, but to the Lord also. The evidence of Mary's commitment must have been satisfying to Jesus. She had been comforted *by* Him; now she was a comfort *to* Him. Isn't that a mind-boggling thought? When you have learned and understood and grown enough, you can give comfort and joy to God Himself.

> When you have learned and understood and grown enough, you can give comfort and joy to God Himself.

May I Have Your Autograph?

A large crowd had gathered outside the house where the party was being held. Like California tourists outside a movie premiere, they were there hoping to see a celebrity. There were two in that house—the man raised from the dead and the Man who raised him. But not everyone in the crowd had benign intentions. Jesus had been a threat to the chief priests; now Lazarus was living proof of the miracle-working power of Jesus. That was a problem; so, they decided to destroy the evidence. They had already decided to kill Jesus, but now they had to get rid of Lazarus too. What irony! Now they were intent on killing the man whom Jesus had raised from the dead.

Everybody Loves a Parade

There was a parade the day after the dinner party. Jesus made His entry into Jerusalem and formally presented Himself to the nation of Israel as the Messiah on what has come to be known as the first Palm Sunday. The crowds responded with an excitement bordering on hysteria. They waved palm fronds torn from trees along the road. As forerunners of Sir Walter Raleigh, they threw their cloaks on the ground for the donkey carrying Jesus to walk on. Traditionally, a king who came in peace rode a donkey; a king who came as a conqueror rode a horse. In every detail Jesus carefully, clearly taught that He came to bring peace to the people who chose to accept His reign over them. To publicly offer Himself to them was an act of sheer courage; He was a wanted man. Though this parade is often referred to as Jesus' "triumphal entry," He wasn't kidding Himself. He knew most people saw Him as a potential political deliverer who would bring freedom from the Roman Empire and social justice. He knew He would die within the week without most of them having comprehended His true mission.

> Jesus carefully, clearly taught that He came to bring peace to the people who chose to accept His reign over them.

The Time Is Right

After He presented Himself at the Temple, some Greeks came asking for an audience. Prior to this, Jesus had offered Himself as Savior and King exclusively to the Jews. This marked a turning point. People outside His own nation began to seek Him out, and He received them.

Since the wedding feast in Cana, Jesus had insisted His "hour had not yet come." Now He said, "The hour has come for the Son of Man to be glorified." (John 12:23) And He proceeded to clearly link His impending death with His coming glorification.

Dying seems an unusual way to be glorified. Jesus offered an illustration from nature as clarification: "[U]nless a kernel of wheat falls to the ground and dies, it remains only a single seed. But if it dies, it produces many seeds." (John 12:24) As life springs from the death of a seed, so life would be the result of the death of Jesus. His physical death would bring spiritual life to many, and that would bring glory to Him and His Father.

Jesus said that when He would be lifted up, He would draw all men to himself. (John 12:32) He said this to show the kind of death He was going to die—lifted up on a cross—crucified. Though Jesus offered Himself to the Jews first, He clearly meant that after His death all races, all nationalities, all kinds of people would be attracted to Him. Like a giant magnet draws iron filings, He will powerfully draw all mankind to Himself. Irresistibly drawn to the magnet, the iron filings cling, not as a result of their own strength, but rather the power of the magnet draws and holds them. However, approached from the wrong angle, a magnet repels; filings literally jump away. So it is with the cross. The cross must be approached correctly, seen not as an antiquated barbaric form of execution with no relevance for modern civilized man, but as a self-sacrificing act of love, with eternal, universal relevance and significance.

> **Like a giant magnet draws iron filings, He will powerfully draw all mankind to Himself.**

How well I remember when I truly committed my life to Christ and wanted to share what I now knew and was experiencing with the whole world! I started with a neighbor. As I shared with her that I at last understood that Jesus' death on the cross followed by His resurrection and ascension was the central, essential message of the gospel, it became very obvious to me she thought the message was totally irrelevant in the 20th century. The Jews expected a political deliverer, not a suffering Savior; therefore, they rejected His work on the cross on their behalf. I'm not sure what many modern-day church goers expect, but I am aware of how irrelevant they find the teaching about Christ's work on the cross. The Apostle Paul predicted this trend in the church long before it happened. He warned young Timothy, whom he was training for ministry, "...the time will come when men will not put up with sound doctrine. Instead, to suit their own desires, they will gather around them a great number of teachers to say what their itching ears want to hear." (2 Timothy 4:3)

Not His powerful teaching, not His amazing miracles, not His life well worthy of emulating, but His death on the cross will ultimately furnish the strongest attraction to the Man called Jesus.

Dear Heavenly Father,

Draw me to Yourself by the power of the cross. Let me truly understand the relevance that the death of Jesus has for me. Use me in a way that will be pleasing to me—and, more importantly, to You! Free me from the inhibitions that prevent my experiencing true worship that will be honoring to You. Amen.

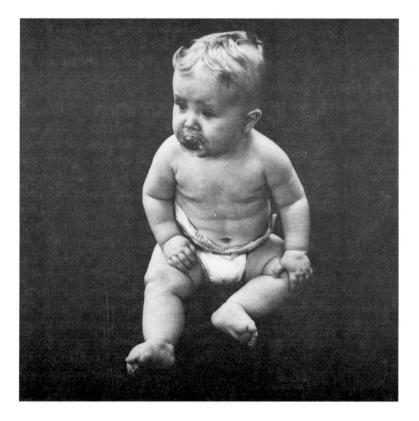

Chapter 13

The Foot Bath

Chapter 13

The Foot Bath

For years I had a wonderful housekeeper who became a dear friend. She was truly a professional in her field and an indispensable part of my life. I will never forget our first meeting. She came highly recommended to me by a friend for whom she worked. It was pretty obvious to Maudie there would soon be another little Larson, as I was about eight months pregnant with my second baby who weighed ten pounds at birth.

Maudie wanted to get some things straight right from the start. "Mrs. Larson," she said, "I don't change diapers, and I don't rinse out dirty diapers. I don't put my hands in the toilet for anybody." Obviously, I had my babies when you still washed diapers unless you were lucky enough to have a diaper service. I assured her that this was my baby and that was my job. She seemed satisfied, and a long, loving relationship between Maudie and our family began.

When Larry was about a month old, I left him with her for an hour while I went to the market. When I got home, she had her hands in the toilet! I was genuinely upset. "Maudie, you could have waited for me; you knew I was coming right back." She insisted that she didn't mind, and I'll never forget how she verbalized the reason for her changed attitude. "Mrs. Larson," she said, "I *love* that baby." And so she did. The years proved she would do anything for him; and he, in turn, would do anything for her because of love. She never had any children of her own, and she loved all four of mine unreservedly. And, oh, how they loved her!

What Is Love?

There is so much disillusionment about love today. The "love children" of the sixties saw the dream of Haight-Ashbury deteriorate into cruelty and bad trips of all kinds. The meaning of the word has itself degenerated because we too often see it characterized on TV commercials as being dependent on or enhanced by the right deodorant, the right toothpaste, the right mouthwash, the right bra, the right whatever—ad nauseum. Or we see unrealistically sentimental or sexy movies and let them define love for us. Moreover, increasing numbers of people are trying out "love" relationships with no commitment. Thus, the meaning of the word is not enhanced but further impoverished.

You may have heard since you were a child that God is love, and indeed He is. Should we not logically expect to learn about real love by looking at the One who is the personification of love?

God Is Love and Jesus Is God

In John's record of the Good News from God, he devotes the last ten chapters to the final seven days of the life of Jesus. Let's take a long look at what is known as the "passion of Christ." John gives few details of the violence that Jesus endured—the account Mel Gibson portrayed so vividly in his movie, *The Passion of the Christ*. I'm almost ashamed to admit that I have never been able to sit all the way through that movie. My nervous system appears to be unable to withstand being exposed to such a reality show featuring the onslaught of such vicious brutality against Jesus. I cry so uncontrollably I have to get up and walk out. I even tried watching the DVD at home so I could more easily leave, calm down, then come back and finish it. I've never made it more than halfway through. Perhaps John, having actually witnessed the merciless cruelty his friend endured, simply could not bring himself to replay that tape.

Jesus' ministry was behind Him now; only a few hours of life remained for Him. His death was so near He was standing figuratively—if not literally—in the shadow of the cross. Yet, the shadow of the cross actually makes Him and His love easier to see.

The shadow of the cross actually makes Him and His love easier to see.

Jesus chose to spend His last hours with His intimate friends, the disciples whom He had trained to carry on His life ministry. He spoke of many things in these waning hours, but His primary emphasis was on love.

John 13:3-5

3   Jesus knew that the Father had put all things under his power, and that he had come from God and was returning to God;

4   so he got up from the meal, took off his outer clothing, and wrapped a towel around his waist.

5   After that, he poured water into a basin and began to wash his disciples' feet, drying them with the towel that was wrapped around him.

Love in Action

John's gospel is the only one which recounts the foot washing incident—a powerful illustration of love in action. It was the custom of the land to have a servant at the door wash the feet of guests as they entered the house. Increasing numbers of 21st century cities are passing laws to protect joggers, runners and just plain walkers from dirty roadways. London's law reads that you must not allow your dog to "foul the footpath."

In the 1st century, no such laws existed. The unpaved streets were used by herds of sheep and goats, horses and donkeys. Those cities had cleaner air, but dirtier roads than modern cities—and everyone wore sandals! No wonder the host didn't wash his guests' feet himself but provided a slave to perform this necessary social amenity.

As the disciples entered the room where the last supper of Jesus' life was to be served, there was no servant. So Jesus, in an unforgettable object lesson, rose from the table and laid aside His outer garment. Clad only in the undergarment that slaves wore, He took a basin and towel and started to wash His disciples' feet.

They were engrossed in a discussion which bordered on being an argument about which one of them was the greatest. This was not the only time the disciples jockeyed for position. Jesus used the incident recorded in Matthew 20:20-28 as a takeoff point for some very challenging teaching on how God views human greatness.

Jesus said, "Whoever wants to become great among you must be your servant, and whoever wants to be first must be your slave.

He said, "Whoever wants to become great among you must be your servant, and whoever wants to be first must be your slave. Just as the Son of Man did not come to be served, but to serve, and to give his life as a ransom for many." I'm afraid most of us are more interested in *hiring* a good servant than *being* a good servant. According to Jesus, that's the wrong emphasis.

Great Enough to Be Humble

Jesus knew exactly who He was: His self image was good; He knew He had value to His Father and to the world. When God gives such security, you can serve others without feeling inferior. A friend of mine in an executive position with a large company regularly makes the coffee and washes the mugs at his office because the secretaries refuse to do so. To be certain that you have value to a corporation or a family or a friend can make you willing to do whatever needs to be done. However, to be sure of your value to God even more effectively changes your idea of what's "beneath your dignity." If you are convinced God has called you to do a certain job, no matter how unfulfilling, no matter how little your talent or training is used, doing it well will give you a sense of fulfillment. Love makes us willing to serve in whatever capacity we are needed.

Love makes us willing to serve in whatever capacity we are needed.

Jesus taught and then illustrated that truth by washing His disciples' feet. Maudie illustrated it too when she rinsed out Larry's diaper. Any mother can tell you from her own experience that she does a lot of things she doesn't enjoy because she loves her child. When you love someone enough, you don't even give it a second thought. I doubt if Jesus even hesitated as He went to fill that basin with water.

It was in the context of the foot washing incident that Jesus gave His disciples what He called "a new commandment."

John 13:34, 35

[34] "A new command I give you: Love one another. As I have loved you, so you must love one another.

[35] By this all men will know that you are my disciples, if you love one another."

126

As the concept of love deteriorates and tends to be equated with sexuality or temporary warm fuzzy feelings, note well that Jesus exhorted His followers to love each other the way He had loved them. And how was that? He had loved them enough to wash their dirty feet—an act of great humility—and within a few hours, He would die for them. In the next chapter, John quotes Jesus as saying, "Greater love has no one than this, that he lay down his life for his friends." (John 15:13) Jesus loved them—and you and me—that much. He died for them—and for us—as an act of great sacrificial love.

One of the things that should distinguish Christians from other people is how we love each other by being willing to serve each other humbly and sacrificially. Observing our capacity for selfless love should draw people to us and, eventually, through us to God.

Peter Puts His Foot in His Mouth

When Jesus said He must wash Peter's feet in order for Peter to have any part with Him, Peter was nonplussed. He was wise enough to realize the impropriety of Jesus washing his feet and brash enough to tell Jesus he wouldn't allow it. How like impulsive Peter! He knew Jesus was God; so he thought that Jesus shouldn't wash his feet. That certainly seemed reasonable. But is it reasonable to think that you can tell God what He should or should not do?

When Jesus rebuked him, Peter immediately went too far the other way and asked to be washed all over. (John13:9) Jesus' reply made it obvious there was an even deeper meaning to the act than to give His disciples an example of selfless service. He told Peter that if he had already had a bath he never needed to be bathed all over again. He just needed to have his feet washed. Obviously, Jesus was not teaching men who lived in that hot climate and walked those dirty roads that they needed but one bath in their lives. This was spiritual teaching. One of the problems He consistently faced was the inability of people to extract the spiritual principle from the material example. One wonders how He kept from saying, "There you go again!"

The cumulative teaching of Scripture is that once our lives and our consciences have been cleansed by faith in Jesus Christ we have been bathed—we are clean. However, the Bible and our own experience also teach that we do make mistakes; we do sin after that initial time of forgiveness. "If we claim to be without sin, we deceive ourselves and the truth is not in us." (1 John 1:8)

Our Feet Get Dirty

Make no mistake about it, this is a dirty world. As we walk through it, our feet get soiled. Too often the world's influence is so insidious, so subtle, and yet so pervasive we don't even realize we are being brainwashed into accepting the world's standards of right and wrong, clean and dirty, instead of God's. One of the ways we do this is to manipulate language. We make a mistake, an error, or have a shortcoming: or, we find a psychological explanation to excuse our behavior. But God has another word for all the ways we fall short of perfection; He calls it *sin*. If you own a Bible, you might want to read the third chapter of the Apostle Paul's letter to the Romans which makes the point that we all sin because we "fall short of the glory of God"—failing to live up to God's perfect standard of righteousness. The word Paul uses which is translated "fall short" is a term used in target practice with a bow and arrow. It simply means you missed the bull's eye.

But God has another word for all the ways we fall short of perfection; He calls it *sin*.

When Paul wrote his letter to the church at Rome, bows and arrows were commonly used weapons of war so the people to whom he wrote would have understood the concept of not hitting the intended target with accuracy. I was an expert with a bow and arrow in high school. I was not a large girl, but I could pull a 40 pound bow. When I let my left arm bend even slightly, the bow string caught me on the inside of my elbow and left a wicked bruise. My coach, instead of criticizing me for "doing that again," would put his hands over mine and show me how to correct the angle—how to get it right. I like to think that's what God does when we miss the mark and suffer painful consequences—He just points out the mistake and helps us correct the error of our ways.

Corrie ten Boom, the Dutch woman who put her own life on the line to save literally thousands of Jews during World War II and who was eventually arrested and survived a German concentration camp, said, "God never forgives an excuse." You must quit making excuses and agree with God that you are not perfect—you missed the bull's eye. You said or did something wrong or maybe you didn't do or say something you should have. You made a mistake. Admit it! You must not stop short. After you agree with Him that you have sinned, you must also agree with Him that *if you have asked*—you are forgiven.

There are many people who bathed years ago, but because of something they have done since are not experiencing His forgiveness. They have wandered away from God and no longer feel close; so they no longer believe they are forgiven. Feelings are completely undependable. You must not let feelings be the basis for your faith. Base your faith on facts, not feelings.

> **Feelings are completely undependable. You must not let feelings be the basis for your faith. Base your faith on facts, not feelings.**

The fact is if you have asked God to forgive you based on what Jesus did for you, you *are* forgiven. You have had a bath; you are clean. Your feet may be dirty from walking around in this world or you may have moved away from God. Even so, God hasn't moved; you have. God has not stopped loving you; you have just stopped feeling His love. God *is* love; He cannot violate His own character; He loves you. Ask Him to forgive you, and He will gladly do so. He is waiting, wanting, wishing to be asked. The pathway back to God is never blocked by God; He is only a prayer away. If you have asked Him to forgive you, you must believe He has. If you have strayed from living a life pleasing to Him since your original plea, just ask Him again and believe that He has granted your request. Remember, you only need one bath. However, to fail to ask to have your feet washed can destroy your joy, your fellowship with God, and even your usefulness to Him.

Jesus died so that you might be washed—forgiven once and for all for failures in your past—*and* forgiven moment by moment for failures since your original bath.

Love Generates Action

Jesus teaches by word and by action that love is active, not passive. Kahlil Gibran in *The Prophet* says "work is love made visible." Few things in that book are scriptural, but I believe that statement is. Jesus expressed love by serving the ones He loved, doing the humblest of tasks on their behalf. He also expressed love by offering up His own life as a sacrificial gift for them and for all of us. In another book John wrote, he defined love by saying, "This is how we know what love is: Jesus Christ laid down His life for us." (1 John 3:16) Our sin makes forgiveness necessary; His death makes forgiveness possible; faith makes forgiveness operative in our lives.

Dear Father in Heaven,

Thank You for loving me. Thank You for sending Jesus to show that love to me. Thank You for the example He showed of sacrificial, serving love. Your love seems all the more wonderful to me because in this world I see so little love that is genuine—that is not distorted, perverted, or self-seeking. Thank You Father and thank You Jesus for Your love. And thank You that when I admit my mistakes to You and ask for Your forgiveness, I not only feel clean, but I am clean. Amen.

Chapter 14

The Last Will and Testament of Jesus

Chapter 14

The Last Will and Testament of Jesus

Jesus had loved His own who were in the world and He now showed them the full extent of His love. The last evening He spent with His disciples He taught them about God's kind of love, both by what He said and what He did. However, the dinner was not a light-hearted love feast. Disturbing things happened; distressing things were said; hearts were heavy.

This group of twelve men had lived, laughed, worked, and prayed together for almost three years. They had literally shared their lives. Now Jesus told them that one of them would betray Him to His enemies and another one would deny his relationship and involvement with Him. And He told them again that He was going to die!

Judas, the one who would betray Him, had already left. The eleven remaining men were despondent, probably distraught. Jesus, though soon to die, was not the one who needed comfort and encouragement. The words Jesus spoke to them are some of the best known, often quoted words in the New Testament. If you have been to a funeral recently you've probably heard them read.

John 14:1-4

1 "Do not let your hearts be troubled. Trust in God; trust also in me.

2 In my Father's house are many rooms; if it were not so, I would have told you. I am going there to prepare a place for you.

3 And if I go and prepare a place for you, I will come back and take you to be with me that you also may be where I am.

4 You know the way to the place where I am going."

Good News and Bad News

Jesus never told any of His followers bad news without immediately telling them good news. He never spoke of His death without speaking of His resurrection. He never let anything seemingly detrimental happen to one of His followers without immediately offering comfort and encouragement.

In this chapter, Jesus used a method of fighting discouragement which is equally sound and satisfactory over 2,000 years later. He reminded the disciples of their faith in God the Father and exhorted them to trust both God the Father and God the Son—even in this situation. He told them that He would return from where He was going to take them to be with Him.

Dr. Richard De Haan, a well known Bible teacher of the 20th century, lived to be a very old man. In the last year of his life he said that Jesus' words, "if it were not so, I would have told you" had become for him the ten most encouraging words in the Bible. After all, Jesus is the Truth. He is not just the personification of Love but also of Truth. God the Son said He would come back for His own, and He will.

Have you ever heard before that Jesus is planning to return? He will come for each of us personally at the time of our departure from this world. But He is not just coming back for us individually. He will eventually return and establish His authority over the earth—an event referred to as the Second Coming. There are twice as many Old Testament prophecies about the second coming of Christ to earth as there are about His first coming. Since those about His first advent have been so literally, specifically fulfilled, it seems logical to assume that those about His second arrival are also accurate and should be believed.

There are twice as many Old Testament prophecies about the second coming of Christ to earth as there are about His first coming.

Home Renovation

Jesus and His disciples had backpacked across Judea and Galilee many times in all kinds of weather. He told them He was going to prepare a mansion for them. No doubt the implication for them was to go from sleeping on that rocky Judean ground to feather mattresses and silk sheets. It's hard to prepare a place for someone else. When our middle son got married, he was living in downtown Los Angeles by the USC Law School. His apartment was roomy and clean, but it urgently needed to be freshened and brightened before he brought his bride there. So, Rick and I spent hours trying to choose some wallpaper for the bathroom and some drapery material for the living room. We finally gave up because when it got right down to the wire, we couldn't decide for Julie how her first apartment should be decorated. I just didn't know her well enough to prepare a place for her that would be sure to please her.

But God knows us! He can call us by name—and that's not all. "And even the very hairs of your head are all numbered." (Matthew 10:30) He knows our ups and downs. (Psalm 139:2) I'm sure He knows that my favorite color is blue and that I love antiques. I often wonder if there will even be antiques in the new heaven and the new earth that the Bible talks about. I surely hope so. But at least I know God knows I don't like stark modern. He's well aware of the fact that I like comfy and cozy. I'm quite sure I'll love what He's preparing for me because *He knows me.* What a thought!

And the landscaping? I can't even imagine how beautiful it will be—roses with no aphids or mildew and lawns with no crab grass. Furthermore, all our loved ones who have preceded us to heaven will be there. There'll be no more tears, no more good-byes, no more misunderstandings, no more trouble communicating—and Jesus will be there!

I'll Be Back!

The phrase "I'll be back" is most remembered in the film *The Terminator* when Arnold Schwarzenegger barged into the police station looking for Sarah Connor whom he planned to "terminate." The policeman at the desk told him that he could not see Sarah because she was giving a statement, but he could sit on the bench and wait. Arnold looked directly at the policeman and emphatically stated, "I'll be back." Minutes later he did come back as he drove his truck into the police station and proceeded to raise havoc with automatic guns searching for his intended prey. The Terminator made good on his promise to return but with devastating results.

When Jesus said He would return He was not making a threat but a promise. His return will bring believers to the place He has prepared for them to spend eternity. His statement brings with it peace and joy and comfort—and truth. There is no doubt that He *can* come back; there is no doubt that He *will* come back. He said He would—and He will!

The Book of Truth

Our natural tendency is to judge the truth of everything in the Bible by our experience instead of judging everything in our experience by the Bible. The basis upon which we believe these things about Heaven and Jesus' return for us is divine revelation. God had them supernaturally written in His book, and He had His book supernaturally preserved.

All the wisdom of the universe is tied up in this one book. Everything we need to know about the origin of life, the history of mankind, the moral and ethical code we should live by right now—it's all there. If there is absolute truth revealed by our Creator, He has a claim on our lives, which should not—*must not*—be denied. We pay a terrible, irrevocably costly price if we choose to ignore His claim.

Love and Obey

Jesus told His disciples, if they loved Him, they would be obedient—they would keep His commandments. If you love someone, you'll want to please them. But how can you know what will please them without their telling you? God has told us in the Bible what actions and attitudes are pleasing to Him. It's as though He has written us a letter.

I went to college in Virginia my freshman year, leaving behind a boy I really cared about. When I got a letter from him, you can be sure I read it. I not only read it, I tried to figure out what would please him based on what he wrote. I poured over those letters. Why? Because I loved him. Should I do less for God Himself? And yet, I did—for years.

The Spirit of Truth

When Jesus told His disciples He was leaving, He not only said He would return, but He promised to send the Holy Spirit to be with them in His place. The Spirit whom He would send would be just like Him, not an inferior version of Him.

Right after World War II when shortages of everything plagued grocery shoppers, I went through the checkout stand at my market directly behind the slightly graying, distinguished, handsome as ever movie star, Walter Pidgeon. (Anybody watch enough old movies on the classic movie channels to know who he is?) The checker asked him if he'd like some pineapple, and in response to his affirmative reply, she surreptitiously produced two cans of Dole pineapple from under the counter. Moments later as she checked my groceries, I casually said, "May I have some pineapple, please?" She responded that there was some on the shelf. "Not like Mr. Pidgeon's," I said. "I don't want an off-brand; I'm not sure of the quality." Sheepishly she produced two more cans of Dole pineapple.

God the Father did not have to be cajoled into giving us someone equal to Himself—He sent His Son. Then, in response to His Son's request, He sent His Holy Spirit. The Holy Spirit is difficult to understand until He actually dwells in you and teaches you.

The Triune God

Verse 16 of John 14 carries a clear reference to all three members of the Trinity: "*I* will ask the *Father*, and he will give you *another counselor.*" The doctrine of the Trinity is essential to the Christian faith, and essential to the doctrine is the fact that God the Father, God the Son, and God the Holy Spirit are one in essence and personality. One is in no way inferior to the other. They play different roles, perform different functions, accept different responsibilities—but they are equal.

The doctrine of the Trinity is essential to the Christian faith.

There is an illustration from the physical world that helped me grasp this difficult concept. The chemical formula for water is H_2O. Whether it appears as liquid, steam, or ice, the equation does not change. Whether the Triune God appears as God the Father, Jesus the Son or the Holy Spirit, the essence is the same.

Sometimes the roles of the three members of the Trinity are so intertwined it is impossible to separate them. In the Old Testament, the Holy Spirit came "upon" kings, princes, and people especially chosen by God to empower them for specific tasks. Jesus promised His disciples and all New Testament believers that the Holy Spirit would come "into" them. He comes "into" you the moment you pray to receive God's forgiveness, because Jesus paid the price for your sin. God's Holy Spirit co-mingles with our spirit; He becomes part of us. He will never leave us, although when God's revealing light shows me yet another change I need to make, I wonder how He can stand some of the things He has had to put up with as He lives in me. He is constantly working to make us what God wants us to be. His job is not only to make each of us a better person here and now, but to prepare us to live in Heaven in the place Jesus has made ready for His loved ones.

His job is not only to make each of us a better person here and now, but to prepare us to live in Heaven.

A Time of Transition

There is no better place in the world to grow up than on a ranch; my childhood was virtually idyllic—an unexcelled preparation for life. However, some facets of my experience were limited. My Texas rancher father had an only brother who was a Texas oilman; they were very different, yet very close. I spent several weeks in the city with my uncle and aunt every summer. They exposed this little country girl to all sorts of new experiences. On the ranch I learned to ride a horse almost before I learned to walk, but in town I finally learned to ride a bike (no sidewalks or paved streets on the ranch). At home I learned to eat fried chicken with my fingers, but in town I learned to eat broiled chicken with a knife and fork—and artichokes and cracked crab. I developed a taste for stage plays and classical music along with rare steak and ripe olives. My relationship with my uncle and aunt changed me and made for a much smoother transition when I eventually moved to a city to live for the rest of my life.

Just so is our relationship with the Holy Spirit; He prepares us for living in a different place for eternity. If we let Him teach us how to deal with our baser instincts, there'll be less culture shock when we move to Heaven.

The Role of the Holy Spirit

Besides making us fit for Heaven, the Holy Spirit has many functions in the life of a believer. Jesus told His disciples that the Holy Spirit would remind them of everything He had said. Those men probably needed very little reminding. Centuries later, as my mind gets cluttered with many things and as my brain ages, I am so grateful that I have the Holy Spirit to help me remember the things that Jesus taught. The Holy Spirit also gives us wisdom, insight and understanding. He gives us power, peace and patience as well as the ability to see the spiritual meaning of our earthly existence.

The whole world clamors for peace. I'm sure even people who do not believe in God yearn for peace—peace in our world, peace in our lives. The Bible teaches there are two kinds of peace available that have nothing to do with the peace in our world. There is peace *with* God referred to in Romans 5:1: "Therefore, since we have been justified through faith, we have peace with God through our Lord Jesus Christ." And there is the peace *of* God referenced in Philippians 4:6, 7: "Do not be anxious about anything, but in everything, by prayer and petition, with thanksgiving, present your requests to God. And the peace of God, which transcends all understanding, will guard your hearts and your minds in Christ Jesus."

The peace *of* God—like the joy of God—is not dependent on circumstances but on the confidence that God is still on the throne and that He will not let anything enter your life experience that you cannot handle if you commit it to Him in prayer and trust Him to walk through it with you. He *will* give you peace—unbelievable, inexplicable, but undeniable peace—peace that doesn't make sense in view of your situation. As Philippians 4:7 says, it does transcend human understanding. However, the verse itself gives some enlightenment as the words Paul used—guard your hearts and your minds—are borrowed from the military terms of his day. What Paul is saying is that Jesus Himself will build a fortress around your heart and mind and protect you

He *will* give you peace— unbelievable, inexplicable, but undeniable peace— peace that doesn't make sense in view of your situation.

from being overwhelmed or defeated by the problems you face. In other words, He will give you a supernatural ability to cope—a peace that is yours because Jesus "willed" it to you.

In the context of the Philippians passage, we find Philippians 4:13 which states: "I can do everything through Him who gives me strength." It is clear from the Bible that the peace *of* God is available only to people who have made their peace *with* God by placing their faith in Jesus Christ and His death on the cross. Once you are a child of God and a citizen of the Kingdom of God, the peace of God is available to you.

Having the Holy Spirit is part of the legacy of being a Christian. Jesus never had a lot of money or a profusion of things, but how good it is to be included in His will and to be endowed with the Holy Spirit and His peace. The riches Jesus left us cannot be consumed by taxes and legal fees; it is ours to claim—it is our inheritance. The whole world yearns for peace, and it is ours to possess; Jesus left it to us. He said, "Peace I leave with you; my peace I give you." (John 14:27)

O God,

Peace, power, patience, love, joy and lots of other things are mine as my inheritance from Jesus—and Your Holy Spirit is in me if I belong to You. I want to make those things part of my experience, not just an unclaimed possession. Why, when He has left me such riches do I act like the will is still held up in probate? If I received an unlimited inheritance of material riches, my natural inclination would undoubtedly be to start "living it up." I do want to claim my spiritual riches and live in such a way that people will at least suspect I'm "nouveau riche." I want to "live it up" for Jesus. Amen

Chapter 15

The Grape Vine

Chapter 15

The Grape Vine

Jesus had a wonderful, down-to-earth way of teaching the truth. He, like the Old Testament writers, used familiar things and common occurrences to illustrate and explain spiritual truths which were somewhat hard to wrap your mind around. His analogies always shed light and give clarity. Who can forget the things He taught about Himself when He said "I am the Bread, the Water, the Light, the Door, the Good Shepherd?" Now He said, "I am the Vine."

John 15:5

5   "I am the vine; you are the branches. If a man remains in me and I in him, he will bear much fruit; apart from me you can do nothing."

On my first trip to Israel I was fascinated to see an excavated carved column in the old synagogue in Capernaum. Built on the foundation of the synagogue where Jesus taught, these ruins date back to the 3rd century. There, chiseled in marble, was a five-pointed star (which has come to be recognized as a Christian star) with a grapevine (which is a symbol of the nation of Israel) entwined around it.

Israel was God's vine. He planted His vine in His vineyard, the world, with the desire that it would be productive and bear fruit. He planned for Israel to record His word, to be the race through which the Savior of the world would be born and to tell the whole world about Him. They did write the Bible, with the exception of two books in the New Testament (Luke who wrote the Gospel of Luke and The Acts of the Apostles was a Gentile), and, of course, Jesus *is* Jewish. However, they failed to share the good news about salvation with the world. Their fruitlessness was a disappointment to God.

Jesus Is the Vine

Jesus, in one concise statement—"I am the Vine"—transferred to Himself all the responsibility and authority that for centuries had belonged exclusively to the nation of Israel. He then enlarged on the metaphor; He is now the vine and those who believe in Him are the branches. Hence, it became the responsibility of that little band of followers and of every believer who followed in their footsteps to share the Good News with the world.

Jesus, in one concise statement—"I am the Vine"—transferred to Himself all the responsibility and authority that for centuries had belonged exclusively to the nation of Israel.

After supper on the last night of His earthly life, Jesus and His disciples left the upstairs room and walked down through a small valley, their way lighted by a full moon. Perhaps Jesus saw a grapevine as He walked. A few grapevines and fig trees still grow there. It was as He crossed the Brook Kidron and climbed the hill on the other side that Jesus taught them using the analogy of the vine and branches.

Jesus told them His Father was the gardener. God Himself was assuming the responsibility formerly held by the religious leaders who had proven themselves to be untrustworthy and incapable. God desires to see fruit; He took charge to ensure results. He will prune, clean, and train the branches so they *will* bear fruit.

The Branches Must Produce Fruit

God's definition of fruit is that of a person drawn to Him because of another believer. Galatians 5:22 speaks of another kind of fruit and gives a list of the "fruit of the Spirit" which includes love, joy, peace, patience, kindness, goodness, faithfulness, gentleness and self-control. This fruit, which delights God, is produced in our characters and personalities.

By effort, you may be able to simulate production of some fruit of the Spirit—and far too many people try. Phony smiles and shallow affection may pass for joy and love, but only temporarily. When artificial fruit made of wax gets too hot, the fact that it is not real becomes apparent. It melts! When our life situation heats up, if our fruit is fake, it will melt away also.

What a Fake

A tour through the Universal Studios in Hollywood is an eye-opener. What appears to be a beautiful structure is often only a façade or an empty shell. If you don't get close enough to see inside, you may not discern the deception. It is the same with Christians who wear masks of spirituality. With some, the deception is conscious and deliberate. They cannot admit they are defeated in their efforts to produce fruit. Others, unknowingly under the influence of a strong human personality or a group of believers, succeed in counterfeiting fruit. They may even deceive themselves temporarily, but they can't fool God. Consider the absurdity of tying ripe peaches on a tree that has produced no fruit in years. A storm of any kind will surely bring them tumbling down.

Whether you are asking God to change your personality, or asking Him to give you a favorable outcome in an assigned task, or asking Him to give you success in sharing your faith, true fruit cannot be produced except in dependence on the Triune God. Jesus said, "Apart from me, you can do nothing." (John 15:5)

> Certainly, you can do things; I had. You can even do good things; I did. However, none of that will count for eternity.

For years that didn't compute for me. What did He mean I could do nothing? I'd been busy all my life. As I grew in understanding, I comprehended the real meaning of that statement. Certainly, you can do things; I had. You can even do good things; I did. However, none of that will count for eternity. That was hard for me to grasp, harder still to accept.

Who Needs the Vine?

I have a good friend whose husband was promoted to a responsible position in one of the major banks in the country. By comparison to his immediate predecessor, he was young. He was also very bright and eager to prove his worth. The first few months were rough. He did not live up to the high standard he had set for his own performance. He was probably more disappointed in himself than his superiors were, but he was hurting. His lovely Christian wife was supportive. She suggested he ask God to help; she intimated the problem might be that he was trying too hard to impress everyone and make a name for himself. She hinted that perhaps he should think more of God's reputation than his own.

During that difficult period my husband and I had dinner with them. He was telling me about her advice. He said, "I'll be honest with you, Dotty. I know I can do this on my own, and I *am* more concerned for my glory than for God's. Is that wrong?"

That was a question which, if I were honest, I'd have to answer affirmatively, and honestly; but I was loathe to do so. He could doubtless answer it for himself by now for he is much more mature in his faith. The logical answer from the human viewpoint is, "Of course, I care about my reputation; I want to make a good name for myself." When we have had a fair degree of success in the world, we know we can do that utilizing our own strengths and abilities. To be told that we cannot do anything without God's power and should not do anything except for God's glory just doesn't sound reasonable.

However, the answer from the divine viewpoint is that we are to ask God for direction not only about what to do but how to do it and then depend on His power to do what He tells us to do. That's hard when you're used to making your own decisions, carrying through on your own and being admired for doing so.

I am so grateful for all the well-meaning, hard-working people who are trying to make the world a better place to live. I hope they don't quit. The world would be much worse without them. In fact, I think if all of them became Christians, most of them would continue doing exactly what they are now doing. However, their motivation and their source of strength would change and so would God's attitude toward their accomplishments. In His eyes, they would become fruit producers and be earning eternal rewards. When Jesus said "Without me you can do nothing," I now understand that He meant nothing of *eternal* significance. Jesus said, "I chose you...to go and bear fruit—fruit that will last." (John 15:16) But He wants us to depend on Him to do that.

God Chose You

You did not choose God; God chose you. Why? Was it because you were so naturally lovely and so wonderfully productive? I guess everything in the world encourages that kind of thinking. As a child in a little school in central Texas, I knew I'd get chosen first for spelling and art memory contests. Outside at recess, I dreaded the choosing for "tug of war" because I really wasn't very strong, and I knew I would be among the last ones chosen. That sort of experience makes you think if you're smart enough or strong enough or useful enough, God will surely choose you. However, God doesn't think like your average fourth grade team captain.

If you can accept the fact that you were chosen because a sovereign God chose to choose you, then you can begin to grasp the concept of a God who loves you and chooses you *in spite of* anything you have done, instead of *because of* anything you have done. Incidentally, having grasped that makes it easier to grapple with and accept the fact that you cannot do anything to make God put you off His team once He's chosen you. You didn't get on the team by being "nasty nice" and you won't be dropped from the roster by "blowing it." Your place on the team is not dependent upon your performance. How different from the world! However, you can forfeit the privilege of being used if you refuse to obey and trust Him.

What Kind of Grapes Are You Growing?

My brother-in-law grew grapes in the Coachella Valley in Southern California. He taught me so much about grapes and thus, unwittingly about my position as a branch. Of course, it's obvious that if a branch is not attached to the vine, it won't bear fruit. However, I did not know that, unlike most other fruit, grapes will not ripen after they are picked. A grape's development stops when it leaves the vine.

We have all tasted sour grapes; we all know Christians who have never matured. A bunch of sour grapes can be thrown away, but immature Christians cannot be discarded so easily. Difficult to work with, unable to carry their fair share of the load, they are a problem to everyone. To people inside the church, they make even the simplest task more emotionally and physically draining. To those outside the church, they often furnish the excuse for remaining outside. The classic example is Huck Finn who said of

> A bunch of sour grapes can be thrown away, but immature Christians cannot be discarded so easily.

Aunt Polly, "If she's going to Heaven I don't want to go there." How clear that makes the importance of staying attached to the vine—of not letting anything interfere with our growing to full turity. God wants His branches to produce sweet fruit; so the first requisite is that we stay attached.

In this analogy Jesus used, it is apparent that the Holy Spirit is the "sap" that must flow freely out from the main vine to and through the branches in order for them to produce fruit. There are innumerable ways we can slow that flow, and our natural personalities mitigate whether we grieve or quench the Holy Spirit. Remember Mary and Martha?

The Father Is the Gardener

Jesus said His Father would personally supervise the trimming of the branches. In the King James Version, the word "pruning" is used. That's a harsher word than trimming. It seems more appropriate to describe some of the things I have experienced since I asked God to see to it that I bore fruit.

Since that day, I have had a complete hysterectomy, a total thyroidectomy, and all the ensuing problems with energy, stamina, and changes in body chemistry those two surgeries can cause. I have also had three major joint replacements, a reaction to what was supposed to be a simple surgery on my hand that precipitated Reflex Sympathetic Dystrophy, and another surgery that was far, far from being simple as it turned into six weeks in the hospital. In addition, we had most of the problems you can think of with raising four teenagers in Southern California in the sixties and seventies, and now three of my four children have experienced broken marriages. At this point I will not even attempt to deal with the deep question of which of those things the Father caused and which He simply allowed. I do now know—both from my study and my personal experience—that God does not see pain the way we do. Years ago someone said, "No pain, no gain." I have been able to accept the fact that some of my most painful experiences have, indeed, been my most gainful ones. I no longer have to know whether God caused something; it is enough to know that God can use it. I am so grateful that I have not only discovered how to claim from Him the strength to endure, but that I have often expe-

rienced the joy of seeing Him use the things He has allowed—even
things that I cannot believe were His
will. To me, the real tragedy is when
pain is wasted because we don't use it
as a platform to tell others of His sufficiency or because we refuse to allow

> It is experiencing God's faithfulness in the midst of our pain that leads us on to maturity.

God to use it as a growing experience in our lives. He does draw
you closer through pain. It is experiencing God's faithfulness in the
midst of our pain that leads us on to maturity.

A Good Crop

There are so many problems in the world that I wonder sometimes how people without a strong faith in a loving God keep from
buckling under the weight of the load. A loving Father will never
allow one of His branches to be pruned in a way that will destroy
it. However, sometimes He does take things out of our lives that
are not bad in themselves. When we come to God, He claims for
Himself all our natural talent and ability, everything our experience
has built into our lives. There's an inherent danger in being naturally gifted. A personal history of achievement without His guidance
and help heightens the inclination to continue in that pattern. God
may have to prune away good, healthy growth to prevent that, but
we will bear more fruit in the long run. Maybe you've never seen a
grapevine that's just been pruned to ensure next year's productivity,
but you must have seen a rose bush pruned so severely you didn't
see how it could even survive, much less ever bloom again. Inevitably the plants bear more fruit, produce more roses because of that
pruning.

I'm sure God loves a profusion of beautiful roses. He likes
grapes too, and He wants them sweet. He has assumed the responsibility of seeing that the branches on His vine produce. In the
King James' Version, John 15:5 says, "He that abideth in me, and I
in him, the same bringeth forth much fruit."

The word "abide" is a rich word. It means more than living in,
dwelling in, remaining in, which are some of the alternate transla-
tions. "To abide" is to settle down and be at home. If we settle
down into God and allow Him to make Himself at home in our
hearts, the "sap" will flow freely and the fruit will come, almost

automatically. The Phillips translation of this verse reads: "It is the man who shares my life and whose life I share who proves fruitful."

Father,

I want to prove fruitful; I want to fulfill Your purpose for my life. Use everything that is part of my life right now—both the joy and the sorrow and pain—to cause me to depend on You more and to produce fruit. Let me personally give evidence of my relationship with You and let others be drawn to You because of who I am, what I say, and what I do. Jesus, You have told us in this chapter to ask for anything in Your name, and so I ask these things in the Name of Jesus. Amen.

Interlude

Do you wonder what it means to ask "in the name of Jesus?" Who has the right to use another person's name?

A child? Yes. Long after I left home when I returned for a visit I could cash a check at the little local grocery store by telling them I was Boone Heep's daughter.

A spouse? Yes. When a love relationship leads to a committed relationship and a man bestows his name on his bride, then she has access to his resources, including a joint bank account.

A legal relationship by power of attorney? Yes. Of course, it is more than obvious that you would never grant your power of attorney to anyone whom you did not trust to always act in your best interest.

So do you have the right to use that name? Are you in the family? Do you have a committed relationship? In the Old Testament God called Israel His wife; in the New Testament He calls the church His bride. Do you think God can trust you to always act in His best interest?

Then use that name—the name of Jesus—when you pray!

Chapter 16

Money in the Bank

Chapter 16

Money in the Bank

When I was a little girl, mother took me with her to the feed store right before Easter. They had a coop full of the cutest, fluffiest little yellow baby chicks I had ever seen. We had a henhouse full of grey-speckled Wyandottes at home, but these were different. I begged for one. Mother acquiesced, and I took my Easter chicken home. Several weeks later when the new had worn off, I tired of giving my little chicken all that personalized care. So, I took it down and released it in the big chicken coop. The next morning I found my little yellow chicken dead—pecked to death by the big gray Wyandottes. She was just too different for them to accept; so they got rid of her.

John 16:1-2

1   "All this I have told you so that you will not go astray.
2   They will put you out of the synagogue; in fact, a time is coming when anyone who kills you will think he is offering a service to God."

Something Different

That's the sort of thing Jesus warned against as He and His disciples walked along through the moonlit night on the way to the Garden of Gethsemane. He cautioned them that when they lived lives pleasing to God, in dependence on the Holy Spirit, they could expect persecution. He wanted them forewarned so they would be forearmed. He told them they should expect hatred; He had experienced it. He warned them that they would be excommunicated from their synagogues, and He told them some would be killed by men who actually thought they were doing God a favor.

History confirms this predicted persecution of the church from the attack leveled against the early church by the Roman Empire to the present persecution of Christians in places such as Russia, China and Iran. If you are His disciple obeying His commandments, you should be different. If you are fortunate enough to have been born in America, you know nothing of suffering imprisonment, atrocities, separation from family, and even death because of your faith in Christ. However, people may laugh at you implying you must not be very smart. Or they may call you homophobic because you believe what the Bible says about homosexuality being contrary to God's plan and thus forbidden. Or you just may not be invited to the neighborhood cocktail party because you talk too much about your new found faith or because your sobriety makes them uncomfortable. In short, they'll try to "peck" you to death. If that happens, remember Jesus told His disciples to anticipate major problems. So, we should not be surprised or unduly disturbed by such minor ones.

John 16:7, 12-14

7 "But I tell you the truth: It is for your good that I am going away. Unless I go away, the Counselor will not come to you; but if I go, I will send him to you.

12 I have much more to say to you, more than you can now bear.

13 But when he, the Spirit of truth, comes, he will guide you into all truth. He will not speak on his own; he will speak only what he hears, and he will tell you what is yet to come.

14 He will bring glory to me by taking from what is mine and making it known to you."

Was Jesus Mistaken?

Jesus' hour had come and the disciples were grieving, but Jesus reminded them it was for their own good that He was leaving because He would send back the Holy Spirit. Another name for the Holy Spirit is the Comforter. I like that! The Holy Spirit was capable of meeting their need for comfort and courage; He is capable of meeting every need of every believer. He'll even help us pray. However, I imagine those eleven unhappy men must have ques-

The Holy Spirit is capable of meeting every need of every believer. He'll even help us pray.

tioned whether Jesus knew what He was talking about when He said it was better for them if He left.

I have a hard time believing that myself sometimes. If only I could share a meal with Jesus and talk to Him, I have thought. Once I received an exciting invitation to a dinner party where Billy Graham was the guest of honor. When we sat down to dinner I could hardly believe my good fortune; the hostess had seated me on his right. My delight turned to disappointment when I realized that the woman seated on his left was vocal about her unbelief and the great evangelist took up the challenge. He spent the entire evening talking to her. That little incident made me realize in a new way how true the words of Jesus were when He said, "It is for your good that I am going away." (John 16:7) What if I had the incredible privilege of dining with Jesus and He talked to the woman on His other side all evening. The Holy Spirit can talk to two women at the same time. Jesus had limitations, albeit self-imposed. However, the Spirit could have been in the kitchen with Martha and out under the fig tree with Mary at the same time. He is God; He is omnipresent.

The Holy Spirit Ministers to Believers

The Holy Spirit is not only a constant companion, He is our teacher. If I were reading a book I didn't understand perfectly and had a chance to ask the author for clarification and interpretation, I would waste no time in doing so. The Holy Spirit inspired and superintended the writing of every word in the Bible; it's His book. He delights in helping us understand it when we ask Him. He will also teach us about Jesus and remind us of truths that we might otherwise forget.

> The Holy Spirit is not only our constant companion, He is our teacher.

Another thing He does for me is to teach me about myself, gradually revealing more and more as I can handle and deal with it. I am grateful He didn't show me everything that needed to be changed in one great revelation. I'm pretty sure I would have been overwhelmed, depressed, and defeated.

And, if you are concerned about the future, the Holy Spirit knows exactly what's going to happen. As time spent listening to

Jesus enabled Mary to understand what Jesus was predicting, so will time spent reading the Bible in dependence on the Holy Spirit give you increased spiritual perception.

The Holy Spirit Ministers to the World

The Holy Spirit's ministry to the world is quite different from His ministry to believers. He will convict the world of sin, convincing those who do not yet believe that the ultimate sin—the *only* unforgivable sin—is to refuse to believe in the saving work of Jesus Christ. He will convince the world that righteousness and morality are not relative, and that there is a perfect standard that is revealed in God's Word, the Bible.

The Holy Spirit will also prove the world wrong in the widely held view that we will never be held accountable—never be judged. Make no mistake about it; there will be a Judgment Day. Satan, the prince of this world, was judged and condemned when Jesus died on the cross. Those who continue in rebellion against God will one day also be judged.

The Bible assures us of the Lord's promise: "My Spirit shall not always strive with man." (Genesis 6:3, KJV) Is God's Spirit still working with you? Oh, how I hope the answer is yes! If it is, I urge you to stop resisting the loving overtures of our patient, pursuing God. "I tell you, now is the time of God's favor, now is the day of salvation." (2 Corinthians 6:2) Tomorrow may be too late.

The Holy Spirit Provides Peace

One of my favorite definitions of peace is having the resources you need when you need them. Before our two oldest sons got married within a month of each other, I spent an inordinate amount of time shopping. The weddings were in two different states; so, I reasoned that if I could find just the right dress for the mother of the groom, I could wear it twice. I did, much to my husband's delight. Finding the right shoes for the dress was almost as hard as finding the dress in the first place. I finally found them, but I had inadvertently left my credit card in another purse. So, I wrote a check. As I headed for the car, I passed the lingerie department and remembered I needed a gift for a personal shower for one of the girls. I found a darling pale pink nightgown; so, I had to write another check. This time the clerk told me I had to go to the credit department to get it approved. The credit department made me wait while they called my bank. My bank said I had insufficient funds to cover the check. At that moment I had no peace!

The next day my husband called the bank, and they assured him it was their mistake. However, that didn't erase my embarrassment or my chagrin at having to go all the way back down Wilshire Blvd. to get that gown which I had, of course, decided was the only one that was just right. Peace is definitely having the resources you need when you need them. When you have the Holy Spirit, you have all the spiritual resources you need at your fingertips all the time.

Peace is definitely having the resources you need when you need them.

Have you ever been to Italy? The name of one of their largest banks is *Banco de Santo Spirito*—the Bank of the Holy Spirit. I am sure people do still write bad checks on that bank, but in God's Bank of the Holy Spirit it is impossible to exhaust the resources available to you. It seems self-evident that when God has supplied such inexhaustible resources for His people we should be invincible. However, few Christians show evidence of experiencing that. Why not?

In Perfect Balance

Many years ago I was having a wonderful visit with my mother and her two sisters when the conversation turned to spiritual things. Aunt Kathryn was always good at asking a key question to stimulate discussion. She asked me what I thought was the greatest problem in the church. While I considered, Aunt Eula spoke up. "I'll tell you what I think," she said. "The Holy Spirit is being neglected. The church needs to teach more about the Holy Spirit and depend on Him more."

She was right. However, in the ensuing years, I think a corresponding error has developed in some parts of the church. While it was and still is true that some fail to put enough emphasis on the Holy Spirit, it is equally true that some over-emphasize His role. The hardest thing in the world to do is to keep your balance.

The Holy Spirit, who is sometimes ignored and sometimes over-emphasized, can give us the balance—even concerning Himself. He is indeed an invaluable gift from God the Father and God the Son. Any good gift from someone who loves you should be used and enjoyed.

Dear Father,

Thank You for warning me about the problems. Thank You for providing the Resource to handle them. I pray for the peace that Jesus promised to be evident in my life because the Holy Spirit is not just present, but in control. Amen.

Chapter 17

A Spiritual Feast

Chapter 17

A Spiritual Feast

I really enjoyed a wonderful trip our family took several years ago. With a name like Larson, it was inevitable that we would eventually go to the Scandinavian countries. The fjords, the forests, the gorgeous scenery—everywhere you looked was so different in that part of the world, a fresh reminder of the diversity of God's creativity. And I loved the different foods! My husband suffered from withdrawal pain because he couldn't get his "two eggs sunny side up with bacon and toast" for breakfast; but I liked the morning buffets with five different kinds of cold meat, three different kinds of cheese, and the wonderful assortment of breads and crackers. And those little sweet rolls—you haven't really had a Danish until you've had a Danish in Denmark!

When I arrived home, my bathroom scales solemnly announced the extent of the damage; so I dutifully went on a diet. Two weeks later we were invited out to dinner. I never like to upset the hostess by not eating, especially when the food is good; so, I nobly—for her sake, of course—broke my diet. I had indigestion all night.

When her life was in a turmoil for several months, our daughter Susie used food to ease her pain. Then her more characteristic self-discipline and determination took over, and she lost forty-five pounds as quickly as she had gained them. She jokingly told me that when all she'd had to eat for days was "a little cottage cheese and a carrot," she had to "go in training" when she intended to start eating again. "You have to work up to eating a lot gradually, Mom, or you'll be sick every time," she warned.

Heavenly Buffet

Arriving at John 17 is like arriving at a banquet, so I hope you are in training, warmed up, and ready to indulge because this is rich! There are people who have been studying their Bibles for years who have not fully digested it. The depth of the passage stretches your mind and your emotions. For a novice at Bible study, spiritual indigestion seems almost inevitable—but, oh, the joy of tasting the riches. I don't get excited about light, airy desserts that obviously include a lot of egg whites in the recipe. I lean toward "heavy" cakes, dark chocolate mousse and rich Crème Brûlée. You've enjoyed a dessert that you knew was too rich, haven't you? Well, get ready to enjoy...

Jesus had repeatedly told His followers He was going to the cross. They had difficulty assimilating that, but Jesus knew He was going to die—and He knew when. Last words always take on added significance, and I am sure Jesus was fully aware of the importance placed on His last words; so, He chose them carefully, thoughtfully.

John 17:1-3

1 After Jesus said this, he looked toward heaven and prayed: "Father, the time has come. Glorify your Son, that your Son may glorify you.

2 For you granted him authority over all people that he might give eternal life to all those you have given him.

3 Now this is eternal life: that they may know you, the only true God, and Jesus Christ, whom you have sent."

Would it embarrass you to inadvertently overhear someone praying? Prayers are so private, so personal. Yet, God the Father chose to make His Son's deep cry to Him public. I never fail to feel a sense of awe and reverence as I read these words for I have been allowed a glimpse, unparalleled elsewhere in Scripture, into the heart and mind of Jesus. He prayed for Himself, speaking of the glory He had with the Father as the pre-existent Christ, the glory He brought the Father by His unreserved obedience, and the glory He was to receive when He returned to the Father. Next, He prayed for His disciples, for their lives to be set apart for God in a special way through the study of the Word of God, for the Father Himself to protect them from the Evil One, and for the Father to give them joy. Last of all, He brought all future believers before the Father's throne and asked that they might experience the same uni-

Prayers are so private, so personal. Yet, God the Father chose to make His Son's deep cry to Him public.

ty that the Triune God experiences and that they might be with Him in Heaven seeing His glory. This brief description doesn't begin to plumb the depths, but, hopefully, you sense that there is hidden treasure that is here waiting to be discovered. Are you willing to dive into deep water?

He Came to Bring Life

One of the things that sustained Jesus in these last hours was His strong sense of identity and mission. He knew who He was; therefore, He could stoop to wash His disciples' feet without losing His dignity. He knew what He came to do—He came to die; therefore, He could face death at His young age without feeling cheated.

My Daddy used to say, "There are only two things I have to do: pay taxes and die." In other words, Daddy recognized there is a sense in which we are all born to die. Death cannot be avoided. Mark Twain noted that the statistics were impressive, "It's 100%. We all die!" he solemnly stated.

> Eternal life is a quantity of life—more importantly, eternal life is a quality of life—most important, eternal life is a relationship with God.

However, Jesus came to die in a different sense; by dying He fulfilled the primary purpose of His life. He came to give eternal life to those who chose to receive it. In order to do that, He had to die to pay the penalty for their sin. Eternal life is a quantity of life—more important, eternal life is a quality of life—most important, eternal life is a relationship with God.

Getting to Know You

I admired Dr. and Mrs. Francis Schaeffer for several years before I met them. He was a gifted man who studied and worked hard to communicate God's truth to modern man, who is caught in the web of today's philosophical thought patterns. With all his brilliance, Dr. Schaeffer escaped appearing cold and clinical because God gave him a heart as big as his brain. His unprepossessing personal appearance, the tremendous drive to do God's will, his superior intellect and deep love for people make me think he and the apostle Paul must be great friends in Heaven. They are definitely kindred spirits.

Dr. Schaeffer's wife, Edith, was divinely suited to be his mate. She shared that rare, remarkable blend of intellect and compassion. I read so much the Schaeffers wrote and heard so much about them from my son, Rick, who studied under him, that I almost felt I knew them. On one of their speaking engagements, I was sitting in the audience when Edith Schaeffer told a story about Rick to illustrate a point. At the conclusion of her speech, I flew down the aisle of the auditorium to identify myself as the mother of the young man she had been talking about. She grasped my hand and invited me to have tea. Two hours later, after feeling for years that I "almost knew her," I really did know her at last. Though I grew to know her better, I really did know her from that very first afternoon.

It is possible to have heard so much about God, read so much He has written as well as what has been written about Him, that you almost feel like you know Him. If you've gotten this far in this book you know a lot about Him now. You may also know a lot of people who have studied under Him and know Him well. You may have even spoken to Him as you read the prayers, but perhaps it's time to stop and ask yourself: do you really have a relationship with God? Jesus came to earth to make that possible. He is the only way to the only God, and if you know Him, you have eternal life. Don't let this moment slip away. Don't let the world's thinking influence you more than it should. Oh sure, there are people whose minds are held captive by a godless world view. Jesus' death on the cross appears to them to be gory, but Jesus considered it glory because it was there He completed the work His Father had given Him to do.

We Need Help

As soon as you have met His Father, Jesus prays for you. He is concerned because He understands the difficulty of living in a world where there is so much evil and where the difference between good and evil is blurred and often obliterated. Malcolm Muggeridge was a brilliant British journalist, author, and media personality who became a Christian late in life. He explained the chaos and cruelty in the world system by comparing it to the havoc it would create in an electrical system if the positives and negatives were reversed. Jesus is concerned not just about the pollution of the air and the water, but of the mind pollution to which we are constantly exposed. Good is still good and bad is still bad, but it's hard to be sure when everyone around you argues it's all relative. We need God's help to think straight. Is it hard for you to admit you need help?

> Good is still good and bad is still bad, but it's hard to be sure when everyone around you argues it's all relative. We need God's help to think straight.

My son Rick and his wife Julie have never had a dog; they are cat people. I, unfortunately, am allergic to cats. So when I visit them I have to stay in a hotel which was always considered a positive, not a negative, by their daughter Marion. By the time she was three, she began staying at the hotel with me. The summer she was four, we went back to the hotel in the afternoon so she could go in the pool. I didn't put my suit on but sat in a chair by the shallow end while she played on the steps. Of course she slipped, and of course she couldn't swim yet. She floated just out of my reach, perfectly perpendicular, her big blue eyes wide open staring at me. Of course, I went in with all my clothes on and fished her out. I held her and hugged her, and she nuzzled my neck for a minute. Then she pushed back and looked me right in the eyes and said very simply, "I needed help." I said, "I know you did, Darling, and I hope I can always be there for you when you need me."

I thought of Jesus' prayer for His future disciples—that's us. We need help. We can't save ourselves. We also need help to discern good and evil, to grow in our faith, and to live in unity with other believers. We don't even have to ask Jesus to pray for us or come to our assistance. I saw that Marion needed help; I jumped in. I am sure that Jesus is just that anxious to help us. He does wait, I think, until we recognize our need for help, but the minute our big scared eyes look to Him, He's in the water with us. He will always be there for us when we need Him.

You Are a Jewel

Remember that famous verse—John 3:16? God loves all the people in this topsy-turvy world so much that He offered them a love gift—His beloved Son. John 17 tells us that He has chosen a gift for this Son He loves so much. If you have accepted the gift of the Son from the Father, you are so special to God that you are now a perfect gift for the Father to give to His Son.

How many times have you heard a teenager say, "I look awful," or "I can't do anything right." Those are ways of saying, "I have no value." A lot of us have never grown up and grown out of that teenage mindset. Eight times in John 17 Jesus exalts believers as He exults over "them you have given me." He is as thrilled as Janet and Julie were with the engagement rings Larry and Rick gave them. Both young men had spent a lot of time, effort, and all the money they could possibly scrape together to get the perfect rings. The girls went around for days holding their hands out for everyone to admire those rings—gifts given in love. Repeatedly, the Bible tells us we are an adornment for Jesus; *we* are *His* jewels. He likes to have us admired.

> If you have accepted the gift of the Son from the Father, you are so special to God that you are now a perfect gift for the Father to give to His Son.

Think about the fact that the "earth is the Lord's and everything in it." (Psalm 24:1) The Father could have given the Son anything He chose to give Him; He owns it all. He could give His Son anything He thought He would like. Ponder this: the Father knows His Son; He knows what pleases Him, and He chose *you*—He chose *me*—as a love gift for Him. Does that do anything for your self esteem? It could—it should. It certainly does great things for mine.

In the Image of God

The balanced truth clearly taught in the Bible is that we are all sinners, and yet we are all made in the image of God. We are not good enough—and self-effort can never make us good enough—to have an intimate relationship with God. When I first heard that, I didn't like it. I didn't like to admit that I needed help. Remember, I hadn't done anything my Grandmother wouldn't be proud to see in the local paper. Later, it became equally difficult for me to experience the opposing truth that I am created in the image of God. Volumes have been written by learned men over many centuries debating what it means to be "made in the image of God." (Genesis 9:6b) I have thoughts on the subject myself, but for now, it is enough to say that whatever it means, it *must* mean—it *has* to mean—that *I* am *wonderful; you* are *wonderful!*

Even without Christ, the human spirit is indomitable—amazing. In the most miserable specimen of the human race there is the capacity to think, to choose, to turn to God, to be restored. As a fine old violin increases in value when it is restored and placed into the hands of a master violinist, so do we increase in value as we are restored to our intended position of fellowship with God. Our increased value is demonstrated to the world as we place ourselves in the hands of the Master. He can make our lives sing, and He prays that we will sing in perfect harmony with other believers.

> Our increased value is demonstrated to the world as we put ourselves in the hands of the Master.

The Perfect Present

What a wonderful gift exchange is described for us in this chapter of John. The Father gave the Son to us. The Father gave us to the Son. The Father promised to send the Holy Spirit because the Son requested Him to do so. For now, the Son promises us productive, fruit-bearing lives and, one day, a home in Heaven. Trouble will come, but joy and peace can be ours because the Father has given us every resource needed to cope. He has given us a new intimate relationship with Himself, and His desire is to give us loving relationships with others.

Has there ever been a Christmas when your children received so many gifts it was almost embarrassing? Well, God spoils His children too. But wouldn't it be disappointing to you if you went to a great deal of trouble and expense to provide special gifts for one of your children, and she was so disinterested she never even bothered to unwrap them... Have you unwrapped your gifts from God?

Dear Father,

It's about time I wrote You a thank you letter. At last I realize how much I have to thank You for. Forgive me for not being properly appreciative sooner. I still have a lot to learn about how to use and enjoy my gifts, but I have made a start, and I'm willing to admit I need help. Thank You so much for making this joy available to me. Thank You for thinking I'm special enough to choose me as a gift for Your Son! I love You, and I do pray, to the best of my ability, in the name of Jesus. Amen.

Interlude

Can you say that prayer with integrity now? Do you love the God who created you? Try saying it over and over—and over and over again. Ask Him to convince you of His love for you if you don't yet feel it. The difficulty of loving someone you cannot see or touch has been discussed many times. When I think of all the gifts He has given me, I feel the love the Father has lavished on me. 1 John 4:19 says we love because He first loved us. If you are still having trouble feeling love for Him, just spend ten minutes every morning and every night for one week concentrating on all He has given you. Thinking of how much He has given you because of His love for you should "jump start" your feeling of love for Him. Your gratitude will just naturally evolve into love.

Chapter 18

A False Arrest

Chapter 18

A False Arrest

Jesus had concluded His final teaching session with His disciples and closed in prayer. As He and His disciples climbed the hill toward an olive grove that belonged to a friend, perhaps they paused and looked back over that beautiful moon-drenched city with its gold and marble Temple. Then they turned and entered the Garden of Gethsemane. They had come often to this quiet place of beauty to rest and to pray.

Jesus again went to His Father in prayer. He was an extremely brave man, but He was not a masochist. The hour for which He had waited all His life had finally come. But, at the human level, He shrank from the well-known excruciating physical pain of death by crucifixion. Perhaps, mercifully, He only suspected the pain of spiritual separation from the Father which He would suffer. Nevertheless, He was almost overcome by the intense emotion he was experiencing.

God Considers His Alternatives

As Jesus prayed, He suffered such agony, such stress, that the capillaries in His skin broke down and blood seeped through the pores. He was deeply troubled. In effect, Jesus asked His Father that night if there was any other way He could complete His life work. God's power is unlimited, but there are self-imposed limitations on when and how He will use it. He will never do anything that violates His own perfect character or His own perfect will. His perfect love desired to find a way to heal the broken relationship and be friends with the humans He created. His perfect righteousness and justice did not allow Him to look the other way and ignore their sin. God had a problem!

My husband used to say that ever since our children were born I had been making excuses for them. I admit that when they were babies and got fussy, I always just blamed it on the fact that they were probably teething. But God doesn't have the freedom to make excuses for us like an overprotective mother. Nor can He pat us on the head and say, "I know you didn't mean to do it" like an overindulgent grandfather. He had to find a way that His justice and love could both be satisfied. His justice demanded payment; His love offered to pay. Even God could find no alternate plan; Jesus had to die to pay the price for our misdeeds, our mistakes, our unkind words, our failures—our sins.

The Struggle to Victory

You cannot come to God by doing enough good things, being generous enough, or even joining the right church. If you could, God the Father could have answered His Son's prayer that night. Jesus didn't want to die; His Father certainly didn't want to require it of Him. But Jesus faced the reality that He must do what He had come to do. He prayed until He was finally able to say, "yet not my will, but yours be done." (Luke 22:42)

He prayed until He was finally able to say, "yet not my will but yours be done."

Joni Erickson Tada, in her first book *Joni*, details her struggle to accept the fact that God had allowed her to be paralyzed from the neck down and that He still had a plan for her life. Now her attitude, her life, her ministry must be a delight to God.

God has allowed trials in my life too, and though they pale in comparison to those Jesus and even Joni faced, there have been some trials, tests and tribulations that I desperately wanted to avoid. Therefore, I have carefully observed how Jesus handled this situation in His life. He labored in prayer that night, pleading with His Father. Yet, the Bible makes it crystal clear that Jesus never sinned. It is such an encouragement to me to know that I can anguish in prayer, asking to be delivered from physical or emotional pain and still be in God's will—for I know to get outside His will is sin.

Dwight L. Moody, a great evangelist of the late 19th century speaking of the difference between being tempted to sin and sinning said, "You can't keep the birds from flying over your head, but you don't have to let them nest in your hair."

What an excellent model of prayer Jesus gives us as He prayed until He reached the place of acceptance—questioning the plan of

God without rebelling against it. I have discovered that works for me too. It's not just a theory that worked for Jesus and for Joni; it's a principle that works for everyone. When I have asked God if He doesn't intend to change the circumstances, then use them to change me, I have experienced a release that is hard to describe by any one word except *victory*.

God let us glimpse the struggle Jesus experienced; then He allowed us to observe Him as, with majestic calm, He proceeded through the evening, protecting His friends and allowing His adversaries to carry out their terrible work.

The Great "I Am"

Jesus' enemies had little in common but their desire to be rid of Him. Opposition to Jesus often does create "strange bed fellows." Normally, the orthodox, conservative Pharisees, the representatives of the high priest and the hated army of occupied Rome were avowed enemies; yet on this mission they cooperated. When they all arrived in the garden, Jesus went out to meet them. He identified Himself in a way that only the initiated would understand was a statement of His deity. In Exodus, the second book of the Old Testament, God called Moses to be His spokesman. Moses protested because he sensed his own inadequacy and asked God what to say when the people to whom he was sent refused to recognize his authority. God told him, "Tell them 'I Am' sent you." (Exodus 3:14) "I Am" is one of the biblical names for God.

When His accusers asked for Jesus of Nazareth, Jesus replied, "I Am" not "I am he" as His response is invariably translated. Those strong, determined men reeled and fell backwards in the face of the majesty and deity of Jesus Christ. With magnificent power and courage, He permitted the actions of the men who had come to arrest Him. They thought they were in the driver's seat when, actually, He had both hands firmly on the wheel.

> Those strong, determined men reeled and fell backwards in the face of the majesty and deity of Jesus Christ.

Say You're Sorry

Peter, on the other hand, was not even in control of himself. His courage was high; his aim was wide. He pulled his sword and barely missed splitting a man's head open, cutting off his ear instead. Jesus miraculously restored the ear and then rebuked Peter for intervening. Jesus' will was now completely submitted to the Father's will. Loyalty to the Father and His plan overruled the human instinct of self-preservation. Not so with Peter!

A few hours before, he had rashly, recklessly told Jesus he would die with Him. Then three times in rapid succession he denied he even knew Him. Jesus had predicted that would happen before the cock crowed to signal the dawning of a new day. Moments after Peter denied his relationship with Jesus for the third time, a rooster crowed. As the first rays of the rising sun streaked the sky with pink, there was no sunshine in Peter's heart. Then as he brooded darkly over how he had failed the Master, Jesus was hustled through the courtyard where he stood. Their eyes met. That one long, loving look from Jesus made him realize the enormity of his failure. And he wept.

Judas, who had betrayed Him for 30 pieces of silver and identified Him to the Roman soldiers with a kiss, realized the consequences of his betrayal. I am sure he also wept tears of frustration and remorse before he hanged himself. (Read Matthew 27:1-10 for the rest of the story.) However, there is a world of difference between the tears of Peter and the tears of Judas. God knows the difference between the two. Tears of remorse say you're sorry things didn't work out; you regret that your plan backfired; you wish you hadn't been caught. Tears of repentance say you are sorry you failed God and with His help you'll try not to make the same mistake again. Tears of remorse say "excuse me;" tears of repentance say "forgive me." Tears of remorse lead to repeated failure; tears of repentance lead to restored fellowship. When you are remorseful, you are filled with self-pity; when you are repentant, you are filled with God. Peter went on to prove his repentance by his fruitful life.

> Tears of remorse say "excuse me;" tears of repentance say "forgive me." Tears of remorse lead to repeated failure; tears of repentance lead to restored fellowship.

A Mockery of Justice

Jesus came to bear witness to the truth. Lying, conniving, evil men put Him on the cross. They made up their minds to kill

Him—the end justified the means. Everything they did to "get" Him was illegal. The Sanhedrin could not legally meet at night, and a meeting could only be called with twenty-four hours advance notice. Yet, the group was hastily assembled that night. Legally, they had to meet in the Temple; yet, they met in the home of the high priest. The Jewish leadership brought no charge against Jesus that could legally be brought before the Roman court. They had no proper witnesses, and they beat a bound prisoner. Everything they did at that trial was in direct conflict with their age-old, God-given code of justice.

> **The Jewish leadership brought no charge against Jesus that could properly be brought before the Roman court.**

They were apparently without scruples. They had made up their minds to kill Jesus and their determination carried them through, although He had done absolutely nothing wrong. Dr. Charles Erdman, a respected professor at Princeton Seminary for many years said, "This is the eternal problem of the enemies of Jesus. Men may hate Him; they may reject Him; they may ignore Him; but actually, they can find nothing to condemn Him. They can never disprove His sinlessness."

The most ironic thing about Jesus' entire life story is that the Jewish religious leaders who plotted to have Him put to death knew the Old Testament Scripture well—even had great portions of it committed to memory—and should have recognized from their own Scriptures that Jesus was their Messiah.

The Picture of the Passover

The Passover Feast celebrated the supernatural protection and deliverance of the Jews when their nation was in bondage in Egypt. The Angel of Death afflicted every house that was not protected by the blood of a slain lamb marked on the doorpost. (Exodus 12) That event foreshadowed the work of Christ. John the Baptist said, "Look, the Lamb of God, who takes away the sin of the world!" (John 1:29) The apostle Paul referred to Jesus as "our Passover lamb." (1 Corinthians 5:7)

It was the Jews' slavish bondage to their own religious ritual that prevented their considering the claims of Christ. Like a small pox vaccination prevents our contracting the disease, our church participation may make us immune to true spirituality. We may get just enough to make us immune to getting the real thing. There is nothing wrong with church or church ritual. There was nothing

Some of us may go to church on Sunday simply to mouth words, parrot prayers and fake faith. wrong with the Passover Feast; it was, in fact, divinely established. Their problem—and often ours—is that we forget the reality behind the ritual. Some of us may go to church on Sunday simply to mouth words, parrot prayers, and fake faith. We actually may come away feeling better. Some who practice religious ritual are lulled into a false sense of security by what is really no more than an habitual performance. Thus, they actually put themselves and their eternal lives in jeopardy. Those Jews held to the form of their worship but rejected the Lord. Dangerous business!

John 18:36-38

36 Jesus said, "My kingdom is not of this world. If it were, my servants would fight to prevent my arrest by the Jews. But now my kingdom is from another place."

37 "You are a king, then!" said Pilate. Jesus answered, "You are right in saying I am a king. In fact, for this reason I was born, and for this I came into the world, to testify to the truth. Everyone on the side of truth listens to me."

38 "What is truth?" Pilate asked. With this he went out again to the Jews and said, "I find no basis for a charge against him."

Just Tell Me the Truth

The Jews brought their rejected Messiah before Pilate. Now Pilate had a problem. His position was tenuous, dependent on his ability to govern those difficult-to-control Jews. He was formerly a Roman slave who had found favor with Caesar's mother-in-law and had been appointed procurator of Israel through her intercession. He needed the cooperation of the Jews in order to maintain the support of the Romans. I'm convinced he longed to know the truth; he asked Jesus the question, "What is truth?" (John 18:38) However, though finding no fault in Jesus, he ultimately forfeited his integrity and protected his position (though history would prove, only briefly) by doing the expedient thing.

Twenty centuries later, Pilate's question remains relevant. "What is truth?" There are many in our century who honestly believe there is no objective truth; truth is relative; truth is nebulous; truth is changing. As a matter of fact, encyclopedias we bought for our children were full of "facts" that are now outdated.

So—what *is* truth? Can it be known? It is my firm conviction that the Bible is God's truth. It is our source of objective, unchanging, eternal truth. It is revealed truth—truth revealed by God. The world needs revealed truth; otherwise, we each determine our own truth and thus our own code of conduct. Terrorists can use children to deliver suicide bombs; their culture holds that to be acceptable. Grown men can be convinced that using young boys as sex toys is acceptable if they join a large group of other men who practice such despicable behavior without compunction. Mothers can take the lives of their unborn babies if giving birth would be inconvenient—and the Supreme Court says it's legal—and thus deemed acceptable. What *is* truth? If there is no revealed truth, no revealed standard of right and wrong, this world is in BIG trouble—*and it is*, in case you haven't noticed!

Where Do You Stand on Truth?

For Pilate, the decision was just too difficult—commitment to the truth too costly. He vacillated, procrastinated, rationalized, compromised his way right into an eternity separated from God. If only he had found truth. If only we would. Jesus said that He was the Truth—absolute perfect truth personified. (John 14:6) Listening to Him will change lives and if enough lives are changed, our world will change.

> Pilate vacillated, procrastinated, rationalized, compromised his way right into an eternity separated from God.

But Pilate took Jesus out to the people, hoping against hope they would let him off the hook. Truth evaded them too. Mob psychology and the fickleness of the human heart worked against both Pilate and Jesus. Less than one week before, perhaps some of those very same people had welcomed Jesus to Jerusalem and shouted, "Hosanna to the King." Now they rejected Him and shouted, "Crucify him...We have no king but Caesar...." (John 19:15) Finally Pilate handed him over to them. Jesus would be crucified.

Pilate made his choice by refusing to make a choice. The Jewish leaders had made their choice. The people had made their choice. Ultimately every person who ever lived must make that same choice. What will *you* do with the revealed Truth of God? What choice will *you* make? What will *you* do with Jesus?

Father God,

I realize life comes as a choice and some choices are not easy. Even after I have made that difficult, all-important choice to believe and receive Jesus, I must choose each moment what course of action I will take, what attitude I should hold, what I accept as truth. Give me the humility to ask for your advice; teach me to look for answers in the Bible. Don't let me get swept along by the crowd. Help me adopt the right world view. Teach my heart to be constant even if some of my family and friends have no understanding of why I have made the choice I have made about Your Son, Jesus. Even if they are very vocal in questioning that choice, give me the courage to take a stand for what I now believe. I ask all this for His sake and for Yours. Amen.

Sins of the World

abandonment ... abominations ... acrimony ... addiction ... adultery ... alcoholism ... animosity ... antagonism ... antipathy ... backbiting ... bad temper ... baseness ... bearing grudges ... betrayal ... bias ... bitterness ... breach of trust ... bribery ... character assassination ... chauvinism ... cheating ... chicanery ... contemptuousness ... corruption ... covetousness ... crime ... criminality ... crookedness ... cunning ... cynicism ... debauchery ... decadence ... deceitfulness ... defamation ... degeneracy ... degradation ... delinquency ... depravity ... discrimination ... dishonesty ... drug abuse ... drunkenness ... duplicity ... enmity ... enslavement ... envy ... eroticism ... evil ... excess ... exploitation ... extortion ... faithlessness ... felony ... fixation ... fornication ... fraud ... gluttony ... gossip ... graft ... greed ... guile ... hate ... hostility ... hypocrisy ... ill-will ... immorality ... impenitence ... inebriation ... infidelity ... infringement ... iniquity ... injustice ... intemperance ... intolerance ... intoxication ... jealousy ... killing ... lack of compassion ... lasciviousness ... lawlessness ... lechery ... lewdness ... libel ... licentiousness ... love of money ... lust ... lying... malevolence ... malfeasance ... malice ... misconduct ... misrepresentation ... narrow-mindedness ... obsession ... one-upmanship ... perjury ... perversion ... pornography ... prayerlessness ... prejudice ... pretense ... pride ... profiteering ... profligacy ... racism ... rage ... rape ... rancor ... resentment ... retribution ... revelry ... revenge ... scandal ... seduction ... self-admiration ... self-gratification ... selfishness ... slander ... spite ... spousal abuse ... taking God's name in vain ... transgression ... treacherousness ... treachery ... treason ... trespasses ... trickery ... unforgivingness ... unrepentance ... unscrupulousness ... vengeance ... verbal abuse ... vice ... viciousness ... villainy ... vindictiveness ... wantonness ... wickedness ... worry ... worshiping false gods ... *and so many more...*

Chapter 19

The Horror of Good Friday

Chapter 19

The Horror of Good Friday

The illegal trials were finished. The well-instructed witnesses with their well-rehearsed stories had been heard. Pilate could find no fault in Jesus, but he could find no daring in himself. Lacking the courage of his convictions, he reluctantly condemned Jesus to death by crucifixion. History can find no justice in his sentence. Originating with the Persians, this form of execution had found its way to the Roman provinces, but it was far too cruel, too barbaric to be used on a Roman citizen. Only slaves and criminals were crucified.

The Day God Died

Jesus was beaten mercilessly by Roman soldiers. Their long leather whips, braided with pieces of sharp bone and metal, were capable of tearing the skin off the victim's bared back. Men often died of shock and blood loss as a result of such a beating before they could be crucified.

John's gospel recounts few details of the death of Christ. We are told only that Jesus was scourged (beaten) and that He carried His own cross to the hill where He died. John was Jesus' cousin and a beloved friend. He saw the whole miserable spectacle. I'm sure the horror—the cruelty almost beyond comprehension—the nightmare of that day was seared into his memory. He never could have forgotten what had happened, but like many battle-tested soldiers, he chose not to talk about what he had seen.

Luke tells us that a group of Jewish women followed Jesus through the streets of Jerusalem "mourning and wailing." (Luke 23:27) Jesus told them not to weep for Him but to weep for themselves and their children. He warned that terrible trials would come to their descendants, a prophecy that has been fulfilled down through the centuries and I believe was partially fulfilled in my lifetime by the atrocities against the Jews perpetrated by Hitler and the Third Reich.

Certainly worth noting is the fact that 25 different prophecies made by many different men over a period of five hundred years between 1,000 and 500 B.C. were fulfilled in 24 hours on the day of Jesus' death.

Prophecies Fulfilled

The Old Testament prophecies tell the story more fully than John does. It was predicted that:

- ✓ Jesus would be betrayed by a friend for thirty pieces of silver which later would be thrown down in the Temple.
- ✓ His disciples would forsake Him.
- ✓ He would be accused by false witnesses.
- ✓ He would be beaten and spat upon, wounded and bruised.
- ✓ He would be crucified with thieves.
- ✓ He would pray for His persecutors.
- ✓ He would be ridiculed by bystanders.
- ✓ His executioners would gamble for His clothing.
- ✓ He would cry out to His Father who had forsaken Him.
- ✓ He would relinquish His own Spirit.
- ✓ There would be darkness over the land.
- ✓ His sword-pierced body—without a broken bone—would be buried in a rich man's tomb.

These and many other incidents which had been predicted happened exactly as forecast. About thirty years ago, *The Passover Plot*, a book discounting the miraculous and accusing Jesus and His disciples of engineering the fulfillment of the prophecies, caused quite a stir. More recently, the alleged "discovery" of the *Gospel of Judas*, which has already been proven to be a hoax, and *The Da Vinci Code*, which certainly proved that Dan Brown is a masterful story teller with a vivid imagination, have received rave reviews in the media and the press. However, Brown's page turner has no more credible facts than the discredited *Gospel of Judas*. Ironically, secular books often impact a thoughtless or gullible public more than they should. Why do we have a tendency to believe what men write more than what God has written?

Actually, it would have been absolutely impossible for Jesus and His followers to contrive or control the fulfillment of these predictions. Do you want to know who choreographed every detail? God the Father ruled that day from start to finish! Jesus influenced the events and people around Him by the sheer force of His majestic personality, and yes, as God, He could have chosen to take control. However, He trusted and submitted to His Father and went to the cross of His own volition.

What Is Your Goal in Life?

Jesus was dedicated to fulfilling God's purpose for His life. Do you yet know what the purpose of your life is? Lots of people have goals, but you can achieve a goal and remain dissatisfied. In *Re-Entry,* John Wesley White states that an incredible number of millionaires commit suicide in the United States every year. If their goal was to make money, when they made it they were not happy and apparently despaired of finding satisfaction any other way.

If you have decided the purpose for your life is to glorify God, you're on the road to happiness. That purpose cannot be thwarted. Even when the circumstances of your life are beyond your control, you can choose to respond in a way that will please and honor God. People can keep you from reaching a goal, but nobody can keep you from fulfilling your purpose if it is to glorify God. Remember that you often cannot control your circumstances, but you always can control your response to them.

Remember that you often cannot control your circumstances, but you always can control your response to them.

Jesus was a Man who kept to His own life plan. He perfectly fulfilled His life's purpose; He glorified God throughout His life and His death. Nevertheless, I find it impossible to comprehend even partially what He experienced those last horrendous hours without feeling gut-wrenching grief and gratitude—and yes— sorrow and sympathy. However, Jesus does not want sympathy. He told the women of Jerusalem not to weep for Him but to weep for themselves and their children because of what would happen to their country due to unbelief. (Luke 23:28) Would He give us the same counsel? Should we be weeping for our ourselves, our children and our grandchildren because of unbelief? What a mess we are leaving for those who follow us!

Take Care of My Mother

Jesus instructed His followers to honor their parents. How could He honor His mother as she stood there watching Him die? He was being put to death because He claimed God was His Father. If she could have named a man as His father, would she not have done so at that moment? She would have brought shame on herself, but she could have saved His life. What mother worthy of that name would even hesitate to make that choice!

John stood nearby, and Jesus asked him, instead of his more immediate family, to care for His mother. John, who was her nephew, took his aunt into his home and provided for her from that day forward. I have been in Ephesus where John spent much of the latter part of his life. Near his tomb stands a lovely little chapel built over the site of the home where Mary lived. As I drank cool water from the well from which she undoubtedly drew her water, I reflected on the wisdom of Jesus. He felt closer to his cousin John who was a true believer than to His own brothers who did not yet accept His deity. He knew John would take good care of her. Jesus was thinking straight even as He was dying on that cross and thus found a way to honor His mother. Mary was so very worthy of honor by Jesus and all of us who love Him. In Jesus' day, single women needed help; so Jesus made provision for her.

However, today, the issue of honoring your parents is a complex one. What of those parents who do not need help or do not appear to deserve honor? What about parents who try to control grown children? Many parents are helping to provide for their children—and grandchildren. We used to tell our children, "As long as you put your feet under our table, we get a vote." So if *they* are helping *you*, you honor them by listening respectfully to their ideas. If *you* are helping *them* and they are manipulative or overly demanding, you need not let them control your life in order to honor them. Give them what they need—not necessarily everything they want.

Shame and Humiliation

Since Adam and Eve hid from God when they recognized their nakedness in the Garden of Eden, public nudity has been considered shameful to God's people. Portrayed in art, the crucified Christ is always discreetly draped. That's not how it was. He hung there naked be-

His being unclothed before them made it possible for us to be clothed before God.

tween two thieves who were crucified with Him. A Jewish man who strictly observed the religious laws could not even participate in the Greek athletic games, forerunner of modern day Olympics, because contestants competed in the nude. I can imagine the shame Jesus felt as He hung there naked, exposed not just before strangers but before His mother and her friends. However, His being unclothed before them made it possible for us to be clothed before God. Even our best efforts to be right and do right can never completely cover our failures—our sin. "[A]ll our righteousnesses are as filthy rags" to God. (Isaiah 64:6, KJV) But, when clothed in the clean, white robes of Christ's righteousness, we are dressed appropriately before God.

When I was in the fourth grade, I rode the bus to school. One rainy day a boy pushed me as I got off the bus. I lost my balance and sprawled in the mud. I was mortified to have to wear that muddy dress all day. Miss Myrtle, my teacher, rescued me. Taking off her own long white sweater, she put it on me and carefully buttoned it up. Because of Christ's death, our defilement—the dirt in our lives—is not just covered up, it is washed away.

John 19:28-30

28 Later, knowing that all was now completed, and so that the Scripture would be fulfilled, Jesus said, "I am thirsty."

29 A jar of wine vinegar was there, so they soaked a sponge in it, put the sponge on a stalk of the hyssop plant, and lifted it to Jesus' lips.

30 When he had received the drink, Jesus said, "It is finished." With that, he bowed his head and gave up his spirit.

A Job Well Done

When Jesus cried out, "It is finished" (John 19:30) as He hung on the cross, He knew He had finished his part of the job of presenting us spotless and blameless before His Father. Moments earlier He had asked for and received a bit of sour wine to clear His throat. Then, He shouted with a strong voice that His work was complete. His last words were not a whimper; He gave a victory cry.

The Greek word He used has been found by archeologists written on the bill of sale of slaves; it is translated "paid in full." When Jesus shouted "It is finished," He was not only announcing that His life work was completed, He was also stating that the charges against you and me have been "paid in full." He bought us out of our slavery to self and sin. We are free! We are clean!

After Jesus triumphantly announced, "It is finished," "He bowed His head and gave up His spirit." (John 19:30b) The original Greek again furnishes an interesting insight. The word translated "bowed" literally means "laid back." Jesus' head did not fall forward in the moment preceding His death as it would naturally have done. Rather, He laid it back on that cross as if it were a pillow. He had not had a place He could call His own since His public ministry began. He said, "Foxes have holes and birds of the air have nests, but the Son of Man has no place to lay his head." (Matthew 8:20) For three years He had not had a place of his own to lay His head. Now, He rested His head on the cross.

The Pain of the Cross

His work completed, Jesus gave up His own life; no one took it from Him. Of His own volition, at the moment of His choosing, He relinquished His Spirit into His Father's hands. The cause of death by crucifixion was usually suffocation as the rib cage collapsed over the diaphragm. Painful as it was to do so, the dying man could push himself up on his spike-torn feet and get slight relief from the agony of dying from the lack of oxygen. Obviously, when the legs were broken, death was hastened.

The religious leaders who were responsible for the death of Jesus asked Pilate to have the prisoners' legs broken so they would die more quickly and could be taken down before the Sabbath began. Pilate yielded to the Jews one more time. When the trained Roman executioner approached the body of Jesus, he saw that He was already dead. Either in an unfeeling act of violence or in an effort to be doubly sure of His death, he stabbed Jesus in the side. There were very few things the Roman executioners and the heartbroken Jewish friends of Jesus could have agreed on that day, but they all agreed that Jesus was definitely dead.

God had allowed the enemies of Jesus to do their worst, but from that moment on, no unfriendly hands touched the body of His beloved Son.

Secret Service Christians

We are not told exactly when Nicodemus acted on the information Jesus gave him the first time they met or when Joseph of Arimathea placed his faith in Christ; but clearly, they were both believers at this point in the story. They were both wealthy members of the Sanhedrin who had been secret followers of Jesus. They had kept their belief a secret for fear of being put out of the synagogue. Being a Secret Service Christian is not really satisfactory—either to you or to God. I am reminded of a placard my son Rick carried in a parade at the height of the Jesus Street People movement. It read, "If you were arrested for being a Christian, would there be enough evidence to convict you?"

Emboldened by the tragic, unjustified execution of their friend, these two Jews "blew their cover" and gave the Jewish leaders enough evidence to convict them of faith in Jesus. They gave Him a burial fit for a king. Using seventy-five pounds of very expensive spices, they wrapped His body and laid it in a new grave that Joseph of Arimathea had purchased in advance for his own burial.

I wondered for years why the day Jesus died is called Good Friday. How could what happened that day be labeled "good?" How can one human be so cruel to another? How can the death of such a good man enhance a day? I realize now that Good Friday is good because of what Jesus accomplished that day. He did what He came to do.

For our sake He endured the indescribable physical torture of crucifixion and the unimaginable emotional stress of temporary separation from His Father. Because of His pain, we can be without the pain of eternal separation from God. Every mother knows the difficulty of physically giving birth to a baby. But, when the baby is longed for, planned for, even prayed for, labor pain seems a minor price to pay for satisfying the longing to hold and love that baby. God has never had an unwanted baby! Jesus chose to suffer so we could be born—spiritually. He completed His labor on Good Friday.

Homesick for Heaven

As Jesus prayed in the Garden of Gethsemane, it is recorded that He was "sorrowful and troubled." (Matthew 26:37) "Troubled" could be accurately translated "homesick." Jesus was homesick for Heaven and for His Father. He could have returned there at any time He chose. However, unless He went by the way of the cross, He would have had to go alone. He had to die to make us holy enough to inhabit Heaven with Him.

He had to die to make us holy enough to inhabit Heaven with Him.

Ropes and nails did not hold Him on that cross—love did! Because of the use He made of it, that cruel instrument of execution has become a symbol of the love of God that is worn as a piece of jewelry by millions. Jesus finished His job on Good Friday. His work, not just for the week, but for His life, was finished. I'm sure He thought, "Thank God, it's Friday!" Now, at last, He could go home.

Our Father Who is in Heaven,

I am glad Jesus is back there with You. I thank You that You loved me enough to send Him to earth. I thank You, Jesus, for loving me enough to return by way of the cross. I thank You, Holy Spirit, for teaching me about these things and for working in me to make me fit for heaven. My heart overflows with love in response to the greatest act of love I have ever encountered. Amen.

Chapter 20

The Glory of Sunday

Chapter 20

The Glory of Sunday

The body of Jesus was hurriedly laid to rest in a burial cave that Joseph of Arimathea had intended to use for himself. The bodies of the poor were usually buried in the ground, the bodies of the rich in caves, not unlike a vault in a mausoleum. A huge stone had been used to close the entrance to Jesus' burial place. The Jewish rulers knew that Jesus had predicted He would return to life, and they feared His disciples might try to steal His body and claim He had made good on His promise to rise from the dead. Therefore, they asked Pilate to post a guard and officially seal the tomb. The scene was set for what Josh McDowell in his book *Evidence That Demands a Verdict* calls "either the greatest miracle or the cruelest hoax" of recorded history.

John 20:1-2

1 Early on the first day of the week, while it was still dark, Mary Magdalene went to the tomb and saw that the stone had been removed from the entrance.

2 So she came running to Simon Peter and the other disciple, the one Jesus loved, and said, "They have taken the Lord out of the tomb, and we don't know where they have put him!"

A Final Service

The grieving disciples had gone into hiding. Before dawn on the first day of the week, Mary Magdalene and the other women headed for the tomb with embalming spices. They appeared to be uninformed about the care already given the body. They expected difficulty in gaining access to the tomb, but their desire to do one last thing for Jesus drove them there.

Several unprecedented events had preceded their arrival. A violent, but apparently localized, earthquake shook the tomb area. An angel with a shining countenance and blinding white robe rolled the stone away from the cave entrance. The guards were so terrified they fainted. When they regained consciousness, they ran into town to report to their superiors. When the women arrived and saw the open tomb, Mary Magdalene immediately ran back to the hideaway of Peter and John. The other women entered the cave, saw the angel, and numbly followed Mary to tell the men of this totally unexpected turn of events.

Give Me a Minute to Think

Mary Magdalene arrived at the men's place of refuge first. With little information and much emotion, she blurted out her hastily drawn conclusion that Jesus' body had been stolen. Close on her heels came the other women. Excitedly they poured out their story of first meeting the angel at the tomb! Thoroughly bewildered, but far too sensible to believe the garbled tale of the women, Peter and John decided to go see for themselves. John was younger and could run faster, so he arrived first but stopped outside the open tomb to catch his breath. Peter, who routinely acted without taking time to catch his breath—or think—rushed right in. The presence of the abandoned grave clothes startled and confused him. John calmly followed him in, took in the whole scene, sized up the situation and arrived at the inescapable conclusion that Jesus Christ had indeed come back from the dead!

The men still had a lot of thinking to do before they understood this was the event that had been predicted in the Old Testament. This was, indeed, what Jesus had repeatedly told them would happen, but their understanding was incomplete. However, John understood enough to believe.

How much do you have to understand to truly believe in Jesus? At what point in a sometimes lengthy courtship by God does a woman yield to His wooing and give her heart to Him? How many nights do you have to lie awake trying to think it through before you are born again? How far do you have to come in your own spiritual pilgrimage before you have arrived?

"I Have Seen the Lord"

The disciples returned to their hideaway. Mary Magdalene returned to the empty tomb. They needed time to think; she needed time to cry. She did not believe the report of the other women any more than the men had. Emotional women with tales of angels and talk of Jesus being alive aren't always believed—even by other women.

Then Mary saw Him! She was crying so hard and the sun was so bright in her eyes that for a moment she didn't recognize Him—until He called her by name.

You'll know Him when He calls you by name! Emotional or unemotional, laughing or crying, determined to doubt or desiring to believe, early in the morning or late at night—you will know Him. His sheep know His voice, and He calls them by name.

That night, still afraid for their lives, ten of the disciples met behind locked doors to discuss the events of the day. Then Jesus appeared in the midst of them. They thought He was a ghost until He spoke to them and showed them His still visible wounds from the spikes and the sword. The Bible says they were overjoyed. That has to be an understatement!

From Doubt to Faith

Thomas was not there that night. He was probably somewhere alone having a pity party. Because he isolated himself from other believers, Thomas had to suffer doubt at least a week longer than necessary. But Jesus came to him, too. Thomas had verbalized what proof he needed.

He knows what we need—which may be something different from what we want.

Jesus didn't even have to read his mind, but He could have. He knows what we need—which may be something different from what we want. He'll give us every proof we *need* to believe.

Thomas made the strongest declaration of faith found in Scripture. That monotheistic Jew, the original "man from Missouri" who had to be shown, said to the Man Jesus, "My Lord and my God!" (John 20:28) "Then Jesus told him, 'Because you have seen me, you have believed; blessed are those who have not seen and yet have believed.'" (John 20:29)

Do you want to receive that blessing? Have you received it? John wrote this entire book for that specific purpose.

John 20:30, 31

³⁰ Jesus did many other miraculous signs in the presence of his disciples, which are not recorded in this book.

³¹ But these are written that you may believe that Jesus is the Christ, the Son of God, and that by believing you may have life in his name.

They'd Rather Die Than Switch

Three fishermen, a tax collector, and an assortment of equally ordinary, unimpressive men huddled in seclusion, afraid for their lives. This unlikely group of men sparked the explosion that shook the world because they saw, they touched, and they talked to the Risen Christ.

The Bible, tradition, and historic accounts combine to give us information about their lives and their deaths. The Apostle John, who cared for Jesus' mother, was the only one of the eleven who lived to be an old man and died a natural death. The other ten died martyrs' deaths. James, the brother of John, was the first to die; Herod had him put to death with the sword. One was boiled in oil; one was tied between two horses and literally torn apart; another was sawn in half. Peter was crucified upside down at his own request because he felt unworthy to die in the same manner as his Lord. Not one of them ever recanted. Not one swerved from his story even though they could have saved their own lives by doing so. They had seen the resurrected Jesus Christ; He was alive. They could not deny the Truth!

What Satisfies You?

We are complex human beings—each composed of mind, emotion and will. In each of us lie infinite possibilities for personality development. To some it is more important to have intellectual questions answered; others deeply desire an emotional experience that will satisfy.

As a brash youth, the Apostle John had a volatile temper; yet, he became the disciple "Jesus loved" (John 20:2) who warmly expressed affection. He also had an analytical mind. Behind every miracle of Jesus that he chronicled, he perceived the deeper meaning. Whenever he described historical events, he explained their symbolic significance. Both sides of his personality were fulfilled through his commitment to Jesus. He was definitely both a left and right brain person.

What Is Faith?

Perhaps because I am a woman, it is important to me to feel my faith. I like to understand what I say I believe; I ask a lot of questions. However, I unashamedly admit my emotions play a role. They did in the faith of Mary Magdalene. Jesus had rescued her from a life of sin, and tears of gratitude, grief, so joy spilled equally easily from her eyes. I can relate to her because I, too, cry easily. However, there is an inherent danger in feeling your faith at the emotional level. The emotions of women go up and down with their hormone count. It's easy to doubt that your faith is genuine when you have a "down" day and don't feel like God is real—or near. I do still have low energy days that are sometimes also low faith days. In Ney Bailey's book, *Faith Is Not a Feeling*, she defines faith this way: "Faith is taking God at His word." Our faith must not be dependent solely on our feelings. If it is to remain stable when something shakes our own private world, it must have a firm foundation. Nor should our decision to believe be a capricious one. It's too easy to doubt the wisdom of snap judgments. An intelligent thoughtful faith is stronger and will serve you better if your smooth sailing suddenly morphs into a rough water ride.

> It's easy to doubt that your faith is genuine when you have a "down" day and don't feel like God is real—or near.

In his book, *In Two Minds*, Oz Guinness deals with "the dilemma of doubt and how to resolve it." He says, "where God has given us sure and sufficient reasons for believing or the possibility of profound understanding in our believing, it is perverse to insist on having less than what he offers."

Most women want to feel things *before* they commit to them; they tend to want their feelings to precede their faith. However, if you know the facts and put your faith in them by an act of your will, feelings will inevitably follow, and your Christian life will feel a lot less like a rollercoaster ride. Facts followed by faith followed by feelings—that will get you a ticket on a smoother ride and the ability to hang on through any turbulence you encounter.

Don't Get Locked Out

Are you a natural born skeptic? We tend to belittle the Apostle Thomas; we've even nicknamed him "doubting Thomas." He wasn't the only one who needed proof of the risen Christ. Eight days earlier Jesus had given the other disciples physical proof on which to build their faith. I admire Thomas for not just taking somebody else's word for it. He did his own digging; he built his own faith. Nevertheless, there is a danger in being a hold-out. It becomes more and more difficult to admit you're wrong, and thus you get locked *into* a position that could get you locked *out of* Heaven.

Jesus didn't criticize Thomas; He never used the derogatory nickname we have given him. Jesus works patiently with each of us. If you have a difficult search, a great struggle, or a long hard pilgrimage, you'll have a stronger faith when the breakthrough finally comes.

Whether you're pragmatic or a philosophical, emotional or stoic, skeptical or gullible, animated or laid back, you can have life in His name. At a moment in time, it *will* come together for you. You may not get all your questions answered; I never have. I simply, by an act of my will, chose to place my faith in God based on the information I had. *I rested my heart in the sufficiency of the facts.* I have never been sorry. Incidentally, the feeling did follow.

Dear God,
As John's gospel draws to a close he reiterates his reason for writing, which was to make sure that anyone who reads his book truly believes that Jesus is the Christ, the Son of God, and thus has life in His name. I want to tell You again I have believed that Jesus is Your unique Son and that He died for me personally. I want my faith to grow stronger. I want to start sharing what I believe with others. I want to be used by You to make our world a better place to live and to leave to our children and grandchildren. I want all this for Christ's sake because of what He did for me. In Jesus' name. Amen.

Chapter 21

A Faith that Saves, Serves, Satisfies

Chapter 21

A Faith that Saves, Serves, Satisfies

When you have truly believed, your life will never be the same. Changes will come—some slowly, some quickly. Peter, who to this point had not exhibited a lot of patience, got tired of waiting on the Lord and decided to go fishing, and four of the other disciples went along; but they didn't catch a single fish.

John 21:4-7

4 Early in the morning, Jesus stood on the shore, but the disciples did not realize that it was Jesus.

5 He called out to them, "Friends, haven't you any fish?" "No," they answered.

6 He said, "Throw your net on the right side of the boat and you will find some." When they did, they were unable to haul the net in because of the large number of fish.

7 Then the disciple whom Jesus loved said to Peter, "It is the Lord!" As soon as Simon Peter heard him say, "It is the Lord," he wrapped his outer garment around him (for he had taken it off) and jumped into the water.

Something Changed

John wrote Chapter 20 to make sure you understand that "Jesus is the Christ, the Son of God, and that by believing you may have life in His name." (John 20:31) He wrote the concluding Chapter 21 apparently to make sure we all understand that saving faith in Christ has great benefits but that it also carries with it great responsibilities. Business as usual won't work. You'll never be able to do your own thing again comfortably or effectively. It didn't work for Peter; it won't work for you; it didn't work for me.

Changed attitudes are the result of faith; actions are the outgrowth of attitudes. If you truly believe in God through Jesus Christ, there *will* be changes—internal and external. Jesus will wait patiently—

Changed attitudes are the result of faith; actions are the outgrowth of attitudes.

sometimes for years—but He *will* get your attention, and He *will* give you directions. If you don't follow them, He'll stay on your case. When you do follow them, He's responsible for the results.

Time for Breakfast

The disciples saw Jesus on the shore, and He told them where to throw their net, which nearly ripped as they tried to haul in their bountiful catch. When they got to the shore, Jesus enjoyed having breakfast with them. The resurrected Jesus had a real body. He was a man, not a phantom. He got hungry, and He ate. He still knew how to start a fire with wet wood. He knew how to clean and cook fish, and He hadn't forgotten how to serve. *He was a man—not an idea, not a concept nor a principle,* as some would have you believe.

Jesus Was Really There

Jesus appeared to the disciples repeatedly—over a period of forty days. They each had their own job to do, their own path to follow, their own journey of faith. He came to them when they were waiting and praying. He came to them when they least expected to see Him. He was teaching them that He was right there even when they could not see or touch Him. He was helping them develop an awareness of His availability to them—to guide and empower them. He taught them that they must each one—individually—follow Him. They were not to question how He chose to work with and through the others. They each had their own job to do, their own path to follow, their own journey of faith. Now that they knew the truth, they must tell others. Once they were built up in their faith, they were able to help build the faith of others. While they might each do it a different way, they always sought His guidance.

We Do Make a Difference

When we took our family to Scotland, my grown boys reverted to childhood. They were determined to go to Loch Ness, and they were even more determined to see the fabled monster Nessie. The day was overcast and the lake was as smooth as glass. No Nessie! They decided if they couldn't see her, at least they would photograph her for friends back home. They spent an hour repeatedly throwing a rock in the lake and trying to snap a picture precisely when it broke the water going down, hoping their picture would appear to show a mysterious creature from the deep breaking the water coming up. My husband and I sat talking, enjoying the spectacular scenery while watching the ripples in the water caused by the rocks the boys threw. Out, out, out they went in ever widening circles.

Don't Be Afraid to Make Waves

Our lives were meant to have an effect on the world. Our desire for public acceptance makes us wary of making waves, or we might hesitate to jump in because we feel we can't make a big enough splash to change anything or influence anybody. Why pay the price of trying when it probably won't accomplish anything anyway—right? However, each of us can—and should—at least make some ripples. Like the ripples originating from a rock thrown in smooth water, our efforts will spread and spread and spread. We may never know where they go, but there *will* be a ripple effect. Because the world we live in and seek to change is rough water, our ripples may not be so easily seen and may seem to quickly disappear. We may get discouraged when we work so hard and see so few results. Even when a little improvement comes, it often seems to dissipate quickly. As a sand castle built on the beach cannot resist the tide, so our best efforts seem unable to survive when hit by the restless sea of the world. But Jesus told us that the things we do in dependence on Him will count for all eternity, and they just might change the world for the better—now!

You Are Chosen

The same God who used that motley crew of men long ago is waiting to use us. He chose them, though they seemed unlikely candidates to change the world so dramatically—

If He chose to choose us, He can choose to use us.

and He chose us. If He chose to choose us, He can choose to use us. The same resurrected Christ who transformed the lives of His disciples is waiting to transform each of us. Once their lives were turned around, they turned the world upside down. The Roman

Empire fell, and slaves were freed because of them. They fought not with guns but with ideas—the ideas of truth and righteousness and justice and freedom. They were armed with love and joy and peace and power from God Himself. We can fight with those same weapons. We have the same God. Do you doubt that our world needs to be turned upside down again?

The World Needs Change

Recently, in a televised interview, I heard the CEO of Google, Eric Schmidt, make the statement that information can change the world. Who would question that the information explosion that has rocked our world for at least the last 30 years has brought about changes—but is the world any better?

Several years ago a research unit funded by the U.S. Office of Education reported that 99% of the students interviewed believed confrontation of some kind is necessary to effectively change society. Clearly our world needs change. It is equally clear that every change is not necessarily for the better. The kind of change needed must come through changed individuals, and an individual can only be changed by a confrontation with the living Christ—there's your "confrontation of some kind" that the students felt was necessary. That confrontation will come when people get the information that God has provided for us in His Word. Therefore, information and confrontation are both necessary for change to take place, but obviously, the right kind of information and the right kind of confrontation are necessary for the right kind of change. Once we accept the Truth about who we are and who Jesus is and what He did for us, then we must allow Him to change us, and then we must work to help Him reach and change others. The result? Our world will be changed—for the better.

John, who wrote this gospel, was a fisherman's son with no education and a hot temper. He became the apostle of love with intense sensitivity to people and the most articulate of men. Saul, the great persecutor of the early church, chose to respond positively to the risen Christ when He appeared to him in a blinding light on the road to Damascus. (Acts 9) He became the great Apostle Paul. He wrote that if anyone was "in Christ" he became a *new* person. (2 Corinthians 5:17) He himself was dramatically changed, yet note well that his zeal, his intelligence, and his education were not erased but rather were re-directed. If Christ has truly come to a-bide—live in—settle down in your heart, your life will be so different; it will be as if you were a *new* person—hence, the "born again" analogy. Yet, God doesn't waste anything. Your tal-

> You can—and should—save soda cans; Jesus can—and does—save people!

ents, training, and experience will endure; but they will be changed and used for His purpose, His glory. The evidence is that Jesus approves of recycling—in all forms. You can—and should—save soda cans; Jesus can—and does—save people!

The Carpenter Is a Potter

The human personality is made of tough material; it is hard to mold, but Jesus Christ can mold it. Then He expects those of us He has worked on to go to work on our world. How do we tap into that power that can change a personality with no propensity for change? How do we make contact with God? Through *faith*.

Although God is a spirit, He is not the only spirit around. That's the reason toying with tarot cards, fortune tellers, or astrology is so dangerous. Many people have been drawn deeply into the occult through such seemingly inane involvement with spirits other than God's Holy Spirit. In retrospect I realize that I almost got drawn into the occult by playing with a Ouija Board when I was a teenager. Faith is like a conductor that connects us to powerful, sometimes shocking forces.

Faith Is...

Faith is not something you choose to have. We all have faith, but we must each choose what we will place our faith in! Faith is operative in our lives on a daily basis. We have faith that the light will come on when we flip the switch; faith that the sun will come up in the morning; faith that the plane will fly; faith that our government will survive; faith that the gas stations will have gas; faith that the supermarket will have turkeys before Thanksgiving; faith that the candy store won't run out of chocolate eggs the day before Easter; faith that our world will continue to spin on its axis; faith in the doctor who prescribes our medicine; faith in the pharmacist

203

who fills the prescriptions—in other words, faith in people and faith in things. We all have faith; yet, the question remains: what is the *object* of our faith?

Hebrews 11:6 says, "And without faith, it is impossible to please God, because anyone who comes to him must believe that he exists and that he rewards those who earnestly seek him." The Gospel of John says, put your faith in God and His Son Jesus Christ. (John 14:1)

In the Beginning

As we come to the end of John's book, let's look again at the beginning. The first chapter opens with some of the most magnificent words in Scripture.

John 1:1-5

1 In the beginning was the Word, and the Word was with God, and the Word was God.

2 He was with God in the beginning.

3 Through him all things were made; without him nothing was made that has been made.

4 In him was life, and that life was the light of men.

5 The light shines in the darkness, but the darkness has not understood it.

If I had been writing the Gospel of John to tell people about Jesus so they could believe—and that is John's stated purpose (John 20:31)—I would not have taken a chance on turning them off right away by declaring that Jesus created the world and everything in it. But that's exactly what John did. You will notice that I did not. I have chosen to use the *beginning* of John's book as the *end* of my book.

There are many similarities between the 1st and 21st centuries: a culture consisting of the very rich and the very poor, rampant sexual immorality, excessive drinking, a great emphasis on education to mention a few. However, in one thing the two centuries differ greatly: *they* recognized that this world did not just accidentally, haphazardly come into existence. Therefore, John didn't even argue for the existence of a god who created; he simply stated that it was Jesus, the Second Person of the Triune Godhead who was the agent of creation.

The Ultimate Communication from God

John called Jesus the Word and then emphatically announced that the Word *was* God. Apart from Him nothing came into existence. Surely that approach was not as likely to turn people off in the 1ˢᵗ century as it is in the 21ˢᵗ century.

Today, the battle over Intelligent Design rages. On one side are those who argue that the irreducible complexity of the smallest cell clearly proves there had to be intelligence involved in its design and creation. They consider it to be scientifically and mathematically impossible for that degree of complexity to simply evolve. On the other side are those who fear that admitting there is intelligent design will inexorably lead to admitting there is a Designer—and that might lead to God, which would be totally unacceptable to them.

> On the other side are those who fear that to admit that there was intelligent design will inexorably lead to admitting there was a designer—and that might lead to God.

John simply chose not to address this problem, which looms so large in our century. After stating that Jesus, the Incarnate Word of God, was the Intelligent Designer of our remarkably complex and beautiful world—and that the world He created rejected Him, he then offers the information that if you believe in and receive Him, you become a child of God. At this point in His record, he makes no further explanation, but simply tells of the beginning of the ministry of Jesus and the call of His disciples. That's where I chose to begin—I didn't want you to stop reading before you really got started.

A Surprising Ally

Way back on June 25, 1978, the *Los Angeles Times* published a lengthy feature story from the pen of Robert Jastrow, an astrophysicist who was at that time the director of NASA's Goddard Institute for Space Studies. He began the article with these words:

"When an astronomer writes about God, his colleagues assume he is either over the hill or going bonkers. In my case they would be mistaken; I am an agnostic in religious matters. However, I am fascinated by some strange developments going on in astronomy—partly because of their religious implications and partly because of the peculiar reactions they have provoked from my colleagues.

"The strange developments are rooted in the growing evidence that the universe had, in some sense, a beginning—that it began at a certain moment in time. Further, that beginning occurred under circumstances that seem to make it impossible—not just now, but ever—to find out what force or forces brought the world into being at that moment. It raised the question of whether the creative agent was one of the familiar forces of physics, or was it, as the Bible says, 'Thine all-powerful hand that creates the world out of formless matter.'" This great agnostic scientist went on record acknowledging the distinct possibility that there was a creative agent who created the world—and it just might have been God.

John clearly states that it *was* Jesus who created the world and Jesus *is* God. Do you choose to believe that Jesus is God and that as God He created the world and everything in it—that you and I didn't just evolve? Do you now believe that God created you and me, that God has a plan for our lives—a *purpose* for *your* life? You don't have to lay aside intellect to believe that, though you may have to lay aside previously held ideas and mindsets.

Why Write Yet Another Book?

John didn't leave anyone guessing about why he wrote his book. He was one of the twelve original disciples of Jesus, and he wrote his gospel after those written by Matthew, Mark and Luke had already been completed and circulated. He did include quite a bit of new material with deeper, clearer insights into the spiritual meaning of the words of Jesus. He wrapped a lot of his instruction around the great "I Am's." Jesus said "I Am the Bread of Life, the Light of the World, the Good Shepherd, the Gate for the sheep, the Resurrection and the Life, the Way and the Truth." So John gives a lot of information about Jesus. However, he clearly stated his *primary* purpose—he wanted people to believe that Jesus was the often-predicted, long-awaited Messiah—the Savior of the world, and he wanted his readers to place their faith in Him. His purpose and mine are synonymous.

This book is quite honestly *not* a commentary on the Gospel of John. Literally hundreds of excellent, erudite commentaries on John have been written. Most of you who have read this book were urged to do so by someone who cares about you. My purpose has been to get anyone who reads it to at least think about the potential difference—the eternal difference—that a vital, operative relationship with God could make in your life.

Joshua Bell is one of the most gifted, accomplished violinists in the world. I recently read about something he did. He put on a pair of jeans and a T-shirt, took his 3.5 million dollar Stradivarius and stood outside the entrance to the L'Enfant Plaza station in Washington, D.C. Standing against a wall next to a trash can he began to play. For close to an hour he serenaded over a thousand people who passed by with beautiful classical music. They ignored him! No one stopped to listen; no one applauded his performance. *They ignored him!* He said later in an interview that it was a very strange feeling to be ignored.

That story stopped me dead in my tracks, for it reminded me of all the years I ignored God. I had prayed and asked for forgiveness as a child. I was convinced of the fact I was a sinner; I had stolen a package of tiny gold pins because I didn't want to learn to work buttonholes on the doll dress I was making. Eaten up by guilt, I hid the pins under a feed sack out in the hay barn. Getting rid of those pins didn't get rid of the conviction that I had done something terribly wrong. My stomach didn't stop hurting. Then on Sunday my whole family went to an evangelistic meeting that just "happened" to be in our small town that week. When an invitation was given to come forward and confess your sins, I was the first one down that aisle.

I knew then that I was forgiven, and I know now that I was accepted by God and adopted into His family as one of His children on that day so long ago. However, I soon forgot the great debt I owed to God's Son for paying the price for my childish failure. For years intellectual pride and "busyness"—those two powerful enemies of a faith that saves, serves, and satisfies encouraged me to ignore God. It must break God's heart when His children do not properly mature. Oh sure, for years I called on God as I raced across the back yard to rescue one of my children as he dangled from the jungle gym or when he took a corner too fast and turned his trike over or when she got so upset she locked herself in her room for hours. Quite honestly, the only time I prayed was when I needed to make a 911 call to God. Most of the time I simply ignored Him! You can ignore Him and never believe or you can believe and then ignore Him. It felt strange to Joshua Bell to be ignored. Can you imagine how it feels to God?

Now as I enjoy this beautiful world He created for His pleasure—and for ours—I always give Him credit. I acknowledge His incredible creative skill. I have literally clapped my hands for Him as I watched an unbelievably beautiful sunset over Manila Bay in the Philippines, and lifted my eyes to Heaven in awe as I saw the "floating" mountain peaks of the Alps break through the clouds in Switzerland, and bowed my head to worship as I held my first great grandson in my arms. I have praised Him as I cut a fragrant bouquet of roses from my own backyard. Mountains and oceans—roses, puppies and babies—zebras, elephants and lions—how *did* He come up with such an absurd, improbable, utterly delightful world? And all the different, wonderful people in my life…He really outdid Himself on people…I thank Him daily for the relationships He has blessed me with!

Don't ignore Him! Tell Him you want Him to be your friend. Set your will on traveling through life with Him at your side. It will totally change your journey!

Dear God,

I acknowledge You and the role You play in my life every moment of every day. Thank You Jesus for introducing me to Your Father. Holy Spirit, help me grow in my faith. Let it be a faith that saves, serves, and satisfies. Thank You, dear God, for being my Guide and my Friend on this lifelong journey into eternity. In the wonderful name of Jesus I earnestly make this request, Amen.

Postlude

By now the name of this book probably needs no explanation. You know that I think that the Christian life is quite a trip! And you know that although life was not designed by God to be lived in isolation, there is a sense in which we all fly solo. We make our own choices—we expedite or delay our own progress. The trip starts with the decision we make about Jesus.

John stated—as you well know by now—that his reason for writing the entire Gospel was so that you may believe that Jesus is the Christ, the Son of God, and that by believing you may have life—eternal life—in His name. John states in Chapter 1 verse 12 that if you receive Jesus into your life and believe in His name, He gives you the right to become a child of God. He reiterates it in Chapter 3 verse 16; there he says that if you believe in Jesus you will never experience separation from God—which he calls perishing—but will have eternal life.

Finally, in Chapter 20 verse 31, John makes his final statement about saving faith; you must believe that Jesus is the Christ, the Son of God, to have life—eternal life. So Flight 2031 is really the last chance to take off for Heaven and the mansion—the eternal home—that Jesus is preparing for you. Needless to say, I hope you haven't missed your flight. You've been offered three different ones: 112, 316 and 2031. The good news is that a flight is never sold out; there is always room on board. In another book that John wrote he said that whoever wished may come. (Revelation 22:17) So if you have decided to take the trip, don't think anything that you did or that happened to you before you made the decision will keep God from issuing your boarding pass. He personally guarantees that you will arrive safely and on time at your eternal destination, and that your old baggage will *not* make the flight if you give Him permission to handle it.

Every summer I took my children home to the ranch where I grew up and inevitably my sister came with her children while we were there. Kathy and Susie always slept together in the big, tall antique four-poster bed in the front bedroom. One night we heard a loud thump followed by an anguished cry. Kathy had fallen out of bed. When we were finally able to quiet her, she explained, "I fell asleep too close to where I got in."

If you are ready to come onboard, get comfortable—but don't go to sleep right away. Too many Christians do that and never progress further to become mature believers. To avoid this pitfall and facilitate personal growth consider some of the following ideas.

Find a church that has a pastor who believes the Bible is the inspired word of God, and start attending that church regularly. See if there is a Community Bible Study, Bible Study Fellowship, or Precepts near you, as these organizations encourage personal study and small group participation. If you are Jewish and have begun to examine Jesus' claim of Messiahship and are ready to embark on a journey of exploration, read Hal Lindsay's, *The Late Great Planet Earth*. Though published in 1970, it has amazingly up-to-date information about God's plan for His chosen people.

If you have a Christian friend, tell her—or him—about your desire to grow and to make friends with other Christians. Friends who encourage you to live a lifestyle that does not reflect your new faith should not be allowed to influence you. You should, instead, try to influence them. Stay close enough to unbelieving friends for communication but not close enough for contamination.

In the Gospel of Matthew, Jesus told His disciples they should be light. Light is a retardant for evil. In other words, our job is to hold back evil by taking a stand for what is right.

Not long ago I stood in my back yard and witnessed a complete lunar eclipse. I was struck again by the fact that all the light of the moon is reflected light from the sun. A lunar eclipse takes place when the world comes between the sun and the moon. As believers, all our light is reflected light from the Son. If we want to be light, as Jesus commanded us to be, we must not let the world come between us and the Son. So beware of the world and its influence! Don't let it come between you and Jesus.

Learn to talk to God honestly and openly—in other words learn to pray. Be serious about growing in your faith but not so serious that you forget that you have embarked on a grand adventure that should give you great joy.

Have a wonderful journey into eternity!

John
(New International Version)

Chapter 1

[1] In the beginning was the Word, and the Word was with God, and the Word was God. [2] He was with God in the beginning.

[3] Through him all things were made; without him nothing was made that has been made. [4] In him was life, and that life was the light of men. [5] The light shines in the darkness, but the darkness has not understood it.

[6] There came a man who was sent from God; his name was John. [7] He came as a witness to testify concerning that light, so that through him all men might believe. [8] He himself was not the light; he came only as a witness to the light. [9] The true light that gives light to every man was coming into the world.

[10] He was in the world, and though the world was made through him, the world did not recognize him. [11] He came to that which was his own, but his own did not receive him. [12] Yet to all who received him, to those who believed in his name, he gave the right to become children of God— [13] children born not of natural descent, nor of human decision or a husband's will, but born of God.

[14] The Word became flesh and made his dwelling among us. We have seen his glory, the glory of the One and Only, who came from the Father, full of grace and truth.

[15] John testifies concerning him. He cries out, saying, "This was he of whom I said, 'He who comes after me has surpassed me because he was before me.'" [16] From the fullness of his grace we have all received one blessing after another. [17] For the law was given through Moses; grace and truth came through Jesus Christ. [18] No one has ever seen God, but God the One and Only, who is at the Father's side, has made him known.

[19] Now this was John's testimony when the Jews of Jerusalem sent priests and Levites to ask him who he was. [20] He did not fail to confess, but confessed freely, "I am not the Christ."

[21] They asked him, "Then who are you? Are you Elijah?"

He said, "I am not."

"Are you the Prophet?"

He answered, "No."

[22] Finally they said, "Who are you? Give us an answer to take back to those who sent us. What do you say about yourself?"

²³ John replied in the words of Isaiah the prophet, "I am the voice of one calling in the desert, 'Make straight the way for the Lord.' "

²⁴ Now some Pharisees who had been sent ²⁵ questioned him, "Why then do you baptize if you are not the Christ, nor Elijah, nor the Prophet?"

²⁶ "I baptize with water," John replied, "but among you stands one you do not know. ²⁷ He is the one who comes after me, the thongs of whose sandals I am not worthy to untie."

²⁸ This all happened at Bethany on the other side of the Jordan, where John was baptizing.

²⁹ The next day John saw Jesus coming toward him and said, "Look, the Lamb of God, who takes away the sin of the world! ³⁰ This is the one I meant when I said, 'A man who comes after me has surpassed me because he was before me.' ³⁰ I myself did not know him, but the reason I came baptizing with water was that he might be revealed to Israel."

³² Then John gave this testimony: "I saw the Spirit come down from heaven as a dove and remain on him. ³³ I would not have known him, except that the one who sent me to baptize with water told me, 'The man on whom you see the Spirit come down and remain is he who will baptize with the Holy Spirit.'³⁴ I have seen and I testify that this is the Son of God."

³⁵ The next day John was there again with two of his disciples. ³⁶ When he saw Jesus passing by, he said, "Look, the Lamb of God!"

³⁷ When the two disciples heard him say this, they followed Jesus. ³⁸ Turning around, Jesus saw them following and asked, "What do you want?"

They said, "Rabbi" (which means Teacher), "where are you staying?"

³⁹ "Come," he replied, "and you will see."

So they went and saw where he was staying, and spent that day with him. It was about the tenth hour.

⁴⁰ Andrew, Simon Peter's brother, was one of the two who heard what John had said and who had followed Jesus. ⁴¹ The first thing Andrew did was to find his brother Simon and tell him, "We have found the Messiah" (that is, the Christ). ⁴² And he brought him to Jesus.

Jesus looked at him and said, "You are Simon son of John. You will be called Cephas" (which, when translated, is Peter).

⁴³ The next day Jesus decided to leave for Galilee. Finding Philip, he said to him, "Follow me."

[44] Philip, like Andrew and Peter, was from the town of Bethsaida. [45] Philip found Nathanael and told him, "We have found the one Moses wrote about in the Law, and about whom the prophets also wrote—Jesus of Nazareth, the son of Joseph."

[46] "Nazareth! Can anything good come from there?" Nathanael asked.

"Come and see," said Philip.

[47] When Jesus saw Nathanael approaching, he said of him, "Here is a true Israelite, in whom there is nothing false."

[48] "How do you know me?" Nathanael asked.

Jesus answered, "I saw you while you were still under the fig tree before Philip called you."

[49] Then Nathanael declared, "Rabbi, you are the Son of God; you are the King of Israel."

[50] Jesus said, "You believe because I told you I saw you under the fig tree. You shall see greater things than that." [51] He then added, "I tell you the truth, you shall see heaven open, and the angels of God ascending and descending on the Son of Man."

Chapter 2

[1] On the third day a wedding took place at Cana in Galilee. Jesus' mother was there, [2] and Jesus and his disciples had also been invited to the wedding. [3] When the wine was gone, Jesus' mother said to him, "They have no more wine."

[4] "Dear woman, why do you involve me?" Jesus replied. "My time has not yet come."

[5] His mother said to the servants, "Do whatever he tells you."

[6] Nearby stood six stone water jars, the kind used by the Jews for ceremonial washing, each holding from twenty to thirty gallons.

[7] Jesus said to the servants, "Fill the jars with water"; so they filled them to the brim.

[8] Then he told them, "Now draw some out and take it to the master of the banquet."

They did so, [9] and the master of the banquet tasted the water that had been turned into wine. He did not realize where it had come from, though the servants who had drawn the water knew. Then he called the bridegroom aside [10] and said, "Everyone brings out the choice wine first and then the cheaper wine after the guests have had too much to drink; but you have saved the best till now."

[11] This, the first of his miraculous signs, Jesus performed at Cana in Galilee. He thus revealed his glory, and his disciples put their faith in him.

[12] After this he went down to Capernaum with his mother and brothers and his disciples. There they stayed for a few days.

[13] When it was almost time for the Jewish Passover, Jesus went up to Jerusalem. [14] In the temple courts he found men selling cattle, sheep and doves, and others sitting at tables exchanging money. [15] So he made a whip out of cords, and drove all from the temple area, both sheep and cattle; he scattered the coins of the money changers and overturned their tables. [16] To those who sold doves he said, "Get these out of here! How dare you turn my Father's house into a market!"

[17] His disciples remembered that it is written: "Zeal for your house will consume me."

[18] Then the Jews demanded of him, "What miraculous sign can you show us to prove your authority to do all this?"

[19] Jesus answered them, "Destroy this temple, and I will raise it again in three days."

[20] The Jews replied, "It has taken forty-six years to build this temple, and you are going to raise it in three days?" [21] But the temple he had spoken of was his body. [22] After he was raised from the dead, his disciples recalled what he had said. Then they believed the Scripture and the words that Jesus had spoken.

[23] Now while he was in Jerusalem at the Passover Feast, many people saw the miraculous signs he was doing and believed in his name. [24] But Jesus would not entrust himself to them, for he knew all men. [25] He did not need man's testimony about man, for he knew what was in a man.

Chapter 3

[1] Now there was a man of the Pharisees named Nicodemus, a member of the Jewish ruling council. [2] He came to Jesus at night and said, "Rabbi, we know you are a teacher who has come from God. For no one could perform the miraculous signs you are doing if God were not with him."

[3] In reply Jesus declared, "I tell you the truth, no one can see the kingdom of God unless he is born again."

[4] "How can a man be born when he is old?" Nicodemus asked. "Surely he cannot enter a second time into his mother's womb to be born!"

[5] Jesus answered, "I tell you the truth, no one can enter the kingdom of God unless he is born of water and the Spirit. [6] Flesh gives birth to

flesh, but the Spirit gives birth to spirit. [7] You should not be surprised at my saying, 'You must be born again.' [8] The wind blows wherever it pleases. You hear its sound, but you cannot tell where it comes from or where it is going. So it is with everyone born of the Spirit."

[9] "How can this be?" Nicodemus asked.

[10] "You are Israel's teacher," said Jesus, "and do you not understand these things? [11] I tell you the truth, we speak of what we know, and we testify to what we have seen, but still you people do not accept our testimony. [12] I have spoken to you of earthly things and you do not believe; how then will you believe if I speak of heavenly things? [13] No one has ever gone into heaven except the one who came from heaven—the Son of Man. [14] Just as Moses lifted up the snake in the desert, so the Son of Man must be lifted up, [15] that everyone who believes in him may have eternal life.

[16] "For God so loved the world that he gave his one and only Son, that whoever believes in him shall not perish but have eternal life. [17] For God did not send his Son into the world to condemn the world, but to save the world through him. [18] Whoever believes in him is not condemned, but whoever does not believe stands condemned already because he has not believed in the name of God's one and only Son. [19] This is the verdict: Light has come into the world, but men loved darkness instead of light because their deeds were evil. [20] Everyone who does evil hates the light, and will not come into the light for fear that his deeds will be exposed. [21] But whoever lives by the truth comes into the light, so that it may be seen plainly that what he has done has been done through God."

[22] After this, Jesus and his disciples went out into the Judean countryside, where he spent some time with them, and baptized. [23] Now John also was baptizing at Aenon near Salim, because there was plenty of water, and people were constantly coming to be baptized. [24] (This was before John was put in prison.) [25] An argument developed between some of John's disciples and a certain Jew over the matter of ceremonial washing. [26] They came to John and said to him, "Rabbi, that man who was with you on the other side of the Jordan—the one you testified about—well, he is baptizing, and everyone is going to him."

[27] To this John replied, "A man can receive only what is given him from heaven. [28] You yourselves can testify that I said, 'I am not the Christ but am sent ahead of him.' [29] The bride belongs to the bridegroom. The friend who attends the bridegroom waits and listens for him, and is full of joy when he hears the bridegroom's voice. That joy is mine, and it is now complete. [30] He must become greater; I must become less.

[30] "The one who comes from above is above all; the one who is from the earth belongs to the earth, and speaks as one from the earth. The one who comes from heaven is above all. [32] He testifies to what he has seen and heard, but no one accepts his testimony. [33] The man who has accepted it has certified that God is truthful. [34] For the one whom God has sent speaks the words of God, for God gives the Spirit without limit. [35] The Father loves the Son and has placed everything in his hands. [36] Whoever believes in the Son has eternal life, but whoever rejects the Son will not see life, for God's wrath remains on him."

Chapter 4

[1] The Pharisees heard that Jesus was gaining and baptizing more disciples than John, [2] although in fact it was not Jesus who baptized, but his disciples. [3] When the Lord learned of this, he left Judea and went back once more to Galilee.

[4] Now he had to go through Samaria. [5] So he came to a town in Samaria called Sychar, near the plot of ground Jacob had given to his son Joseph. [6] Jacob's well was there, and Jesus, tired as he was from the journey, sat down by the well. It was about the sixth hour.

[7] When a Samaritan woman came to draw water, Jesus said to her, "Will you give me a drink?" [8] (His disciples had gone into the town to buy food.)

[9] The Samaritan woman said to him, "You are a Jew and I am a Samaritan woman. How can you ask me for a drink?" (For Jews do not associate with Samaritans.)

[10] Jesus answered her, "If you knew the gift of God and who it is that asks you for a drink, you would have asked him and he would have given you living water."

[11] "Sir," the woman said, "you have nothing to draw with and the well is deep. Where can you get this living water? [12] Are you greater than our father Jacob, who gave us the well and drank from it himself, as did also his sons and his flocks and herds?"

[13] Jesus answered, "Everyone who drinks this water will be thirsty again, [14] but whoever drinks the water I give him will never thirst. Indeed, the water I give him will become in him a spring of water welling up to eternal life."

[15] The woman said to him, "Sir, give me this water so that I won't get thirsty and have to keep coming here to draw water."

[16] He told her, "Go, call your husband and come back."

[17] "I have no husband," she replied.

Jesus said to her, "You are right when you say you have no husband. [18] The fact is, you have had five husbands, and the man you now have is not your husband. What you have just said is quite true."

[19] "Sir," the woman said, "I can see that you are a prophet. [20] Our fathers worshiped on this mountain, but you Jews claim that the place where we must worship is in Jerusalem."

[21] Jesus declared, "Believe me, woman, a time is coming when you will worship the Father neither on this mountain nor in Jerusalem. [22] You Samaritans worship what you do not know; we worship what we do know, for salvation is from the Jews. [23] Yet a time is coming and has now come when the true worshipers will worship the Father in spirit and truth, for they are the kind of worshipers the Father seeks. [24] God is spirit, and his worshipers must worship in spirit and in truth."

[25] The woman said, "I know that Messiah" (called Christ) "is coming. When he comes, he will explain everything to us."

[26] Then Jesus declared, "I who speak to you am he."

[27] Just then his disciples returned and were surprised to find him talking with a woman. But no one asked, "What do you want?" or "Why are you talking with her?"

[28] Then, leaving her water jar, the woman went back to the town and said to the people, [29] "Come, see a man who told me everything I ever did. Could this be the Christ?" [30] They came out of the town and made their way toward him.

[30] Meanwhile his disciples urged him, "Rabbi, eat something."

[32] But he said to them, "I have food to eat that you know nothing about."

[33] Then his disciples said to each other, "Could someone have brought him food?"

[34] "My food," said Jesus, "is to do the will of him who sent me and to finish his work. [35] Do you not say, 'Four months more and then the harvest'? I tell you, open your eyes and look at the fields! They are ripe for harvest. [36] Even now the reaper draws his wages, even now he harvests the crop for eternal life, so that the sower and the reaper may be glad together. [37] Thus the saying 'One sows and another reaps' is true. [38] I sent you to reap what you have not worked for. Others have done the hard work, and you have reaped the benefits of their labor."

[39] Many of the Samaritans from that town believed in him because of the woman's testimony, "He told me everything I ever did." [40] So when the Samaritans came to him, they urged him to stay with them, and he

stayed two days. [41] And because of his words many more became believers.

[42] They said to the woman, "We no longer believe just because of what you said; now we have heard for ourselves, and we know that this man really is the Savior of the world."

[43] After the two days he left for Galilee. [44] (Now Jesus himself had pointed out that a prophet has no honor in his own country.) [45] When he arrived in Galilee, the Galileans welcomed him. They had seen all that he had done in Jerusalem at the Passover Feast, for they also had been there.

[46] Once more he visited Cana in Galilee, where he had turned the water into wine. And there was a certain royal official whose son lay sick at Capernaum. [47] When this man heard that Jesus had arrived in Galilee from Judea, he went to him and begged him to come and heal his son, who was close to death.

[48] "Unless you people see miraculous signs and wonders," Jesus told him, "you will never believe."

[49] The royal official said, "Sir, come down before my child dies."

[50] Jesus replied, "You may go. Your son will live."

The man took Jesus at his word and departed. [51] While he was still on the way, his servants met him with the news that his boy was living. [52] When he inquired as to the time when his son got better, they said to him, "The fever left him yesterday at the seventh hour."

[53] Then the father realized that this was the exact time at which Jesus had said to him, "Your son will live." So he and all his household believed.

[54] This was the second miraculous sign that Jesus performed, having come from Judea to Galilee.

Chapter 5

[1] Some time later, Jesus went up to Jerusalem for a feast of the Jews. [2] Now there is in Jerusalem near the Sheep Gate a pool, which in Aramaic is called Bethesda and which is surrounded by five covered colonnades. [3] Here a great number of disabled people used to lie—the blind, the lame, the paralyzed. [5] One who was there had been an invalid for thirty-eight years. [6] When Jesus saw him lying there and learned that he had been in this condition for a long time, he asked him, "Do you want to get well?"

[7] "Sir," the invalid replied, "I have no one to help me into the pool when the water is stirred. While I am trying to get in, someone else goes down ahead of me."

[8] Then Jesus said to him, "Get up! Pick up your mat and walk." [9] At once the man was cured; he picked up his mat and walked.

The day on which this took place was a Sabbath, [10] and so the Jews said to the man who had been healed, "It is the Sabbath; the law forbids you to carry your mat."

[11] But he replied, "The man who made me well said to me, 'Pick up your mat and walk.'"

[12] So they asked him, "Who is this fellow who told you to pick it up and walk?"

[13] The man who was healed had no idea who it was, for Jesus had slipped away into the crowd that was there.

[14] Later Jesus found him at the temple and said to him, "See, you are well again. Stop sinning or something worse may happen to you." [15] The man went away and told the Jews that it was Jesus who had made him well.

[16] So, because Jesus was doing these things on the Sabbath, the Jews persecuted him. [17] Jesus said to them, "My Father is always at his work to this very day, and I, too, am working." [18] For this reason the Jews tried all the harder to kill him; not only was he breaking the Sabbath, but he was even calling God his own Father, making himself equal with God.

[19] Jesus gave them this answer: "I tell you the truth, the Son can do nothing by himself; he can do only what he sees his Father doing, because whatever the Father does the Son also does. [20] For the Father loves the Son and shows him all he does. Yes, to your amazement he will show him even greater things than these. [21] For just as the Father raises the dead and gives them life, even so the Son gives life to whom he is pleased to give it. [22] Moreover, the Father judges no one, but has entrusted all judgment to the Son, [23] that all may honor the Son just as they honor the Father. He who does not honor the Son does not honor the Father, who sent him.

[24] "I tell you the truth, whoever hears my word and believes him who sent me has eternal life and will not be condemned; he has crossed over from death to life. [25] I tell you the truth, a time is coming and has now come when the dead will hear the voice of the Son of God and those who hear will live. [26] For as the Father has life in himself, so he has granted the Son to have life in himself. [27] And he has given him authority to judge because he is the Son of Man.

[28] "Do not be amazed at this, for a time is coming when all who are in their graves will hear his voice [29] and come out—those who have done good will rise to live, and those who have done evil will rise to be con-

demned. [30] By myself I can do nothing; I judge only as I hear, and my judgment is just, for I seek not to please myself but him who sent me.

[30] "If I testify about myself, my testimony is not valid. [32] There is another who testifies in my favor, and I know that his testimony about me is valid.

[33] "You have sent to John and he has testified to the truth. [34] Not that I accept human testimony; but I mention it that you may be saved. [35] John was a lamp that burned and gave light, and you chose for a time to enjoy his light.

[36] "I have testimony weightier than that of John. For the very work that the Father has given me to finish, and which I am doing, testifies that the Father has sent me. [37] And the Father who sent me has himself testified concerning me. You have never heard his voice nor seen his form, [38] nor does his word dwell in you, for you do not believe the one he sent. [39] You diligently study the Scriptures because you think that by them you possess eternal life. These are the Scriptures that testify about me, [40] yet you refuse to come to me to have life.

[41] "I do not accept praise from men, [42] but I know you. I know that you do not have the love of God in your hearts. [43] I have come in my Father's name, and you do not accept me; but if someone else comes in his own name, you will accept him. [44] How can you believe if you accept praise from one another, yet make no effort to obtain the praise that comes from the only God?

[45] "But do not think I will accuse you before the Father. Your accuser is Moses, on whom your hopes are set. [46] If you believed Moses, you would believe me, for he wrote about me. [47] But since you do not believe what he wrote, how are you going to believe what I say?"

Chapter 6

[1] Some time after this, Jesus crossed to the far shore of the Sea of Galilee (that is, the Sea of Tiberias), [2] and a great crowd of people followed him because they saw the miraculous signs he had performed on the sick. [3] Then Jesus went up on a mountainside and sat down with his disciples. [4] The Jewish Passover Feast was near.

[5] When Jesus looked up and saw a great crowd coming toward him, he said to Philip, "Where shall we buy bread for these people to eat?" [6] He asked this only to test him, for he already had in mind what he was going to do.

[7] Philip answered him, "Eight months' wages would not buy enough bread for each one to have a bite!"

⁸ Another of his disciples, Andrew, Simon Peter's brother, spoke up, ⁹ "Here is a boy with five small barley loaves and two small fish, but how far will they go among so many?"

¹⁰ Jesus said, "Have the people sit down." There was plenty of grass in that place, and the men sat down, about five thousand of them. ¹¹ Jesus then took the loaves, gave thanks, and distributed to those who were seated as much as they wanted. He did the same with the fish.

¹² When they had all had enough to eat, he said to his disciples, "Gather the pieces that are left over. Let nothing be wasted." ¹³ So they gathered them and filled twelve baskets with the pieces of the five barley loaves left over by those who had eaten.

¹⁴ After the people saw the miraculous sign that Jesus did, they began to say, "Surely this is the Prophet who is to come into the world." ¹⁵ Jesus, knowing that they intended to come and make him king by force, withdrew again to a mountain by himself.

¹⁶ When evening came, his disciples went down to the lake, ¹⁷ where they got into a boat and set off across the lake for Capernaum. By now it was dark, and Jesus had not yet joined them. ¹⁸ A strong wind was blowing and the waters grew rough. ¹⁹ When they had rowed three or three and a half miles, they saw Jesus approaching the boat, walking on the water; and they were terrified. ²⁰ But he said to them, "It is I; don't be afraid." ²¹ Then they were willing to take him into the boat, and immediately the boat reached the shore where they were heading.

²² The next day the crowd that had stayed on the opposite shore of the lake realized that only one boat had been there, and that Jesus had not entered it with his disciples, but that they had gone away alone. ²³ Then some boats from Tiberias landed near the place where the people had eaten the bread after the Lord had given thanks. ²⁴ Once the crowd realized that neither Jesus nor his disciples were there, they got into the boats and went to Capernaum in search of Jesus.

²⁵ When they found him on the other side of the lake, they asked him, "Rabbi, when did you get here?"

²⁶ Jesus answered, "I tell you the truth, you are looking for me, not because you saw miraculous signs but because you ate the loaves and had your fill. ²⁷ Do not work for food that spoils, but for food that endures to eternal life, which the Son of Man will give you. On him God the Father has placed his seal of approval."

²⁸ Then they asked him, "What must we do to do the works God requires?"

²⁹ Jesus answered, "The work of God is this: to believe in the one he has sent."

³⁰ So they asked him, "What miraculous sign then will you give that we may see it and believe you? What will you do? ³⁰ Our forefathers ate the manna in the desert; as it is written: 'He gave them bread from heaven to eat.'"

³² Jesus said to them, "I tell you the truth, it is not Moses who has given you the bread from heaven, but it is my Father who gives you the true bread from heaven. ³³ For the bread of God is he who comes down from heaven and gives life to the world."

³⁴ "Sir," they said, "from now on give us this bread."

³⁵ Then Jesus declared, "I am the bread of life. He who comes to me will never go hungry, and he who believes in me will never be thirsty. ³⁶ But as I told you, you have seen me and still you do not believe. ³⁷ All that the Father gives me will come to me, and whoever comes to me I will never drive away. ³⁸ For I have come down from heaven not to do my will but to do the will of him who sent me. ³⁹ And this is the will of him who sent me, that I shall lose none of all that he has given me, but raise them up at the last day. ⁴⁰ For my Father's will is that everyone who looks to the Son and believes in him shall have eternal life, and I will raise him up at the last day."

⁴¹ At this the Jews began to grumble about him because he said, "I am the bread that came down from heaven." ⁴² They said, "Is this not Jesus, the son of Joseph, whose father and mother we know? How can he now say, 'I came down from heaven'?"

⁴³ "Stop grumbling among yourselves," Jesus answered. ⁴⁴ "No one can come to me unless the Father who sent me draws him, and I will raise him up at the last day. ⁴⁵ It is written in the Prophets: 'They will all be taught by God.' Everyone who listens to the Father and learns from him comes to me. ⁴⁶ No one has seen the Father except the one who is from God; only he has seen the Father. ⁴⁷ I tell you the truth, he who believes has everlasting life. ⁴⁸ I am the bread of life. ⁴⁹ Your forefathers ate the manna in the desert, yet they died. ⁵⁰ But here is the bread that comes down from heaven, which a man may eat and not die. ⁵¹ I am the living bread that came down from heaven. If anyone eats of this bread, he will live forever. This bread is my flesh, which I will give for the life of the world."

⁵² Then the Jews began to argue sharply among themselves, "How can this man give us his flesh to eat?"

⁵³ Jesus said to them, "I tell you the truth, unless you eat the flesh of the Son of Man and drink his blood, you have no life in you. ⁵⁴ Whoever eats my flesh and drinks my blood has eternal life, and I will raise him up at the last day. ⁵⁵ For my flesh is real food and my blood is real drink. ⁵⁶

Whoever eats my flesh and drinks my blood remains in me, and I in him. [57] Just as the living Father sent me and I live because of the Father, so the one who feeds on me will live because of me. [58] This is the bread that came down from heaven. Your forefathers ate manna and died, but he who feeds on this bread will live forever." [59] He said this while teaching in the synagogue in Capernaum.

[60] On hearing it, many of his disciples said, "This is a hard teaching. Who can accept it?"

[61] Aware that his disciples were grumbling about this, Jesus said to them, "Does this offend you? [62] What if you see the Son of Man ascend to where he was before! [63] The Spirit gives life; the flesh counts for nothing. The words I have spoken to you are spirit and they are life. [64] Yet there are some of you who do not believe." For Jesus had known from the beginning which of them did not believe and who would betray him. [65] He went on to say, "This is why I told you that no one can come to me unless the Father has enabled him."

[66] From this time many of his disciples turned back and no longer followed him.

[67] "You do not want to leave too, do you?" Jesus asked the Twelve.

[68] Simon Peter answered him, "Lord, to whom shall we go? You have the words of eternal life. [69] We believe and know that you are the Holy One of God."

[70] Then Jesus replied, "Have I not chosen you, the Twelve? Yet one of you is a devil!" [71] (He meant Judas, the son of Simon Iscariot, who, though one of the Twelve, was later to betray him.)

Chapter 7

[1] After this, Jesus went around in Galilee, purposely staying away from Judea because the Jews there were waiting to take his life. [2] But when the Jewish Feast of Tabernacles was near, [3] Jesus' brothers said to him, "You ought to leave here and go to Judea, so that your disciples may see the miracles you do. [4] No one who wants to become a public figure acts in secret. Since you are doing these things, show yourself to the world." [5] For even his own brothers did not believe in him.

[6] Therefore Jesus told them, "The right time for me has not yet come; for you any time is right. [7] The world cannot hate you, but it hates me because I testify that what it does is evil. [8] You go to the Feast. I am not yet going up to this Feast, because for me the right time has not yet come." [9] Having said this, he stayed in Galilee.

^{10} However, after his brothers had left for the Feast, he went also, not publicly, but in secret. ^{11} Now at the Feast the Jews were watching for him and asking, "Where is that man?"

^{12} Among the crowds there was widespread whispering about him. Some said, "He is a good man."

Others replied, "No, he deceives the people." ^{13} But no one would say anything publicly about him for fear of the Jews.

^{14} Not until halfway through the Feast did Jesus go up to the temple courts and begin to teach. ^{15} The Jews were amazed and asked, "How did this man get such learning without having studied?"

^{16} Jesus answered, "My teaching is not my own. It comes from him who sent me. ^{17} If anyone chooses to do God's will, he will find out whether my teaching comes from God or whether I speak on my own. ^{18} He who speaks on his own does so to gain honor for himself, but he who works for the honor of the one who sent him is a man of truth; there is nothing false about him. ^{19} Has not Moses given you the law? Yet not one of you keeps the law. Why are you trying to kill me?"

^{20} "You are demon-possessed," the crowd answered. "Who is trying to kill you?"

^{21} Jesus said to them, "I did one miracle, and you are all astonished. ^{22} Yet, because Moses gave you circumcision (though actually it did not come from Moses, but from the patriarchs), you circumcise a child on the Sabbath. ^{23} Now if a child can be circumcised on the Sabbath so that the law of Moses may not be broken, why are you angry with me for healing the whole man on the Sabbath? ^{24} Stop judging by mere appearances, and make a right judgment."

^{25} At that point some of the people of Jerusalem began to ask, "Isn't this the man they are trying to kill? ^{26} Here he is, speaking publicly, and they are not saying a word to him. Have the authorities really concluded that he is the Christ? ^{27} But we know where this man is from; when the Christ comes, no one will know where he is from."

^{28} Then Jesus, still teaching in the temple courts, cried out, "Yes, you know me, and you know where I am from. I am not here on my own, but he who sent me is true. You do not know him, ^{29} but I know him because I am from him and he sent me."

^{30} At this they tried to seize him, but no one laid a hand on him, because his time had not yet come. ^{30} Still, many in the crowd put their faith in him. They said, "When the Christ comes, will he do more miraculous signs than this man?"

³² The Pharisees heard the crowd whispering such things about him. Then the chief priests and the Pharisees sent temple guards to arrest him.

³³ Jesus said, "I am with you for only a short time, and then I go to the one who sent me. ³⁴ You will look for me, but you will not find me; and where I am, you cannot come."

³⁵ The Jews said to one another, "Where does this man intend to go that we cannot find him? Will he go where our people live scattered among the Greeks, and teach the Greeks? ³⁶ What did he mean when he said, 'You will look for me, but you will not find me,' and 'Where I am, you cannot come'?"

³⁷ On the last and greatest day of the Feast, Jesus stood and said in a loud voice, "If anyone is thirsty, let him come to me and drink. ³⁸ Whoever believes in me, as the Scripture has said, streams of living water will flow from within him." ³⁹ By this he meant the Spirit, whom those who believed in him were later to receive. Up to that time the Spirit had not been given, since Jesus had not yet been glorified.

⁴⁰ On hearing his words, some of the people said, "Surely this man is the Prophet."

⁴¹ Others said, "He is the Christ."

Still others asked, "How can the Christ come from Galilee? ⁴² Does not the Scripture say that the Christ will come from David's family and from Bethlehem, the town where David lived?" ⁴³ Thus the people were divided because of Jesus. ⁴⁴ Some wanted to seize him, but no one laid a hand on him.

⁴⁵ Finally the temple guards went back to the chief priests and Pharisees, who asked them, "Why didn't you bring him in?"

⁴⁶ "No one ever spoke the way this man does," the guards declared.

⁴⁷ "You mean he has deceived you also?" the Pharisees retorted. ⁴⁸ "Has any of the rulers or of the Pharisees believed in him? ⁴⁹ No! But this mob that knows nothing of the law—there is a curse on them."

⁵⁰ Nicodemus, who had gone to Jesus earlier and who was one of their own number, asked, ⁵¹ "Does our law condemn anyone without first hearing him to find out what he is doing?"

⁵² They replied, "Are you from Galilee, too? Look into it, and you will find that a prophet does not come out of Galilee."

⁵³ Then each went to his own home.

Chapter 8

¹ But Jesus went to the Mount of Olives. ² At dawn he appeared again in the temple courts, where all the people gathered around him, and he sat down to teach them. ³ The teachers of the law and the Pharisees brought in a woman caught in adultery. They made her stand before the group ⁴ and said to Jesus, "Teacher, this woman was caught in the act of adultery. ⁵ In the Law Moses commanded us to stone such women. Now what do you say?" ⁶ They were using this question as a trap, in order to have a basis for accusing him.

But Jesus bent down and started to write on the ground with his finger. ⁷ When they kept on questioning him, he straightened up and said to them, "If any one of you is without sin, let him be the first to throw a stone at her." ⁸ Again he stooped down and wrote on the ground.

⁹ At this, those who heard began to go away one at a time, the older ones first, until only Jesus was left, with the woman still standing there. ¹⁰ Jesus straightened up and asked her, "Woman, where are they? Has no one condemned you?"

¹¹ "No one, sir," she said.

"Then neither do I condemn you," Jesus declared. "Go now and leave your life of sin."

¹² When Jesus spoke again to the people, he said, "I am the light of the world. Whoever follows me will never walk in darkness, but will have the light of life."

¹³ The Pharisees challenged him, "Here you are, appearing as your own witness; your testimony is not valid."

¹⁴ Jesus answered, "Even if I testify on my own behalf, my testimony is valid, for I know where I came from and where I am going. But you have no idea where I come from or where I am going. ¹⁵ You judge by human standards; I pass judgment on no one. ¹⁶ But if I do judge, my decisions are right, because I am not alone. I stand with the Father, who sent me. ¹⁷ In your own Law it is written that the testimony of two men is valid. ¹⁸ I am one who testifies for myself; my other witness is the Father, who sent me."

¹⁹ Then they asked him, "Where is your father?"

"You do not know me or my Father," Jesus replied. "If you knew me, you would know my Father also." ²⁰ He spoke these words while teaching in the temple area near the place where the offerings were put. Yet no one seized him, because his time had not yet come.

²¹ Once more Jesus said to them, "I am going away, and you will look for me, and you will die in your sin. Where I go, you cannot come."

²² This made the Jews ask, "Will he kill himself? Is that why he says, 'Where I go, you cannot come'?"

²³ But he continued, "You are from below; I am from above. You are of this world; I am not of this world. ²⁴ I told you that you would die in your sins; if you do not believe that I am the one I claim to be, you will indeed die in your sins."

²⁵ "Who are you?" they asked.

"Just what I have been claiming all along," Jesus replied. ²⁶ "I have much to say in judgment of you. But he who sent me is reliable, and what I have heard from him I tell the world."

²⁷ They did not understand that he was telling them about his Father. ²⁸ So Jesus said, "When you have lifted up the Son of Man, then you will know that I am the one I claim to be and that I do nothing on my own but speak just what the Father has taught me. ²⁹ The one who sent me is with me; he has not left me alone, for I always do what pleases him." ³⁰ Even as he spoke, many put their faith in him.

³⁰ To the Jews who had believed him, Jesus said, "If you hold to my teaching, you are really my disciples. ³² Then you will know the truth, and the truth will set you free."

³³ They answered him, "We are Abraham's descendants and have never been slaves of anyone. How can you say that we shall be set free?"

³⁴ Jesus replied, "I tell you the truth, everyone who sins is a slave to sin. ³⁵ Now a slave has no permanent place in the family, but a son belongs to it forever. ³⁶ So if the Son sets you free, you will be free indeed. ³⁷ I know you are Abraham's descendants. Yet you are ready to kill me, because you have no room for my word. ³⁸ I am telling you what I have seen in the Father's presence, and you do what you have heard from your father."

³⁹ "Abraham is our father," they answered.

"If you were Abraham's children," said Jesus, "then you would do the things Abraham did. ⁴⁰ As it is, you are determined to kill me, a man who has told you the truth that I heard from God. Abraham did not do such things. ⁴¹ You are doing the things your own father does."

"We are not illegitimate children," they protested. "The only Father we have is God himself."

⁴² Jesus said to them, "If God were your Father, you would love me, for I came from God and now am here. I have not come on my own; but he sent me. ⁴³ Why is my language not clear to you? Because you are unable to hear what I say. ⁴⁴ You belong to your father, the devil, and you want to carry out your father's desire. He was a murderer from the begin-

ning, not holding to the truth, for there is no truth in him. When he lies, he speaks his native language, for he is a liar and the father of lies. ⁴⁵ Yet because I tell the truth, you do not believe me! ⁴⁶ Can any of you prove me guilty of sin? If I am telling the truth, why don't you believe me? ⁴⁷ He who belongs to God hears what God says. The reason you do not hear is that you do not belong to God."

⁴⁸ The Jews answered him, "Aren't we right in saying that you are a Samaritan and demon-possessed?"

⁴⁹ "I am not possessed by a demon," said Jesus, "but I honor my Father and you dishonor me. ⁵⁰ I am not seeking glory for myself; but there is one who seeks it, and he is the judge. ⁵¹ I tell you the truth, if anyone keeps my word, he will never see death."

⁵² At this the Jews exclaimed, "Now we know that you are demon-possessed! Abraham died and so did the prophets, yet you say that if anyone keeps your word, he will never taste death. ⁵³ Are you greater than our father Abraham? He died, and so did the prophets. Who do you think you are?"

⁵⁴ Jesus replied, "If I glorify myself, my glory means nothing. My Father, whom you claim as your God, is the one who glorifies me. ⁵⁵ Though you do not know him, I know him. If I said I did not, I would be a liar like you, but I do know him and keep his word. ⁵⁶ Your father Abraham rejoiced at the thought of seeing my day; he saw it and was glad."

⁵⁷ "You are not yet fifty years old," the Jews said to him, "and you have seen Abraham!"

⁵⁸ "I tell you the truth," Jesus answered, "before Abraham was born, I am!" ⁵⁹ At this, they picked up stones to stone him, but Jesus hid himself, slipping away from the temple grounds.

Chapter 9

¹ As he went along, he saw a man blind from birth. ² His disciples asked him, "Rabbi, who sinned, this man or his parents, that he was born blind?"

³ "Neither this man nor his parents sinned," said Jesus, "but this happened so that the work of God might be displayed in his life. ⁴ As long as it is day, we must do the work of him who sent me. Night is coming, when no one can work. ⁵ While I am in the world, I am the light of the world."

⁶ Having said this, he spit on the ground, made some mud with the saliva, and put it on the man's eyes. ⁷ "Go," he told him, "wash in the

Pool of Siloam" (this word means Sent). So the man went and washed, and came home seeing.

[8] His neighbors and those who had formerly seen him begging asked, "Isn't this the same man who used to sit and beg?" [9] Some claimed that he was.

Others said, "No, he only looks like him."

But he himself insisted, "I am the man."

[10] "How then were your eyes opened?" they demanded.

[11] He replied, "The man they call Jesus made some mud and put it on my eyes. He told me to go to Siloam and wash. So I went and washed, and then I could see."

[12] "Where is this man?" they asked him.

"I don't know," he said.

[13] They brought to the Pharisees the man who had been blind. [14] Now the day on which Jesus had made the mud and opened the man's eyes was a Sabbath. [15] Therefore the Pharisees also asked him how he had received his sight. "He put mud on my eyes," the man replied, "and I washed, and now I see."

[16] Some of the Pharisees said, "This man is not from God, for he does not keep the Sabbath."

But others asked, "How can a sinner do such miraculous signs?" So they were divided.

[17] Finally they turned again to the blind man, "What have you to say about him? It was your eyes he opened."

The man replied, "He is a prophet."

[18] The Jews still did not believe that he had been blind and had received his sight until they sent for the man's parents. [19] "Is this your son?" they asked. "Is this the one you say was born blind? How is it that now he can see?"

[20] "We know he is our son," the parents answered, "and we know he was born blind. [21] But how he can see now, or who opened his eyes, we don't know. Ask him. He is of age; he will speak for himself." [22] His parents said this because they were afraid of the Jews, for already the Jews had decided that anyone who acknowledged that Jesus was the Christ would be put out of the synagogue. [23] That was why his parents said, "He is of age; ask him."

[24] A second time they summoned the man who had been blind. "Give glory to God," they said. "We know this man is a sinner."

[25] He replied, "Whether he is a sinner or not, I don't know. One thing I do know. I was blind but now I see!"

[26] Then they asked him, "What did he do to you? How did he open your eyes?"

[27] He answered, "I have told you already and you did not listen. Why do you want to hear it again? Do you want to become his disciples, too?"

[28] Then they hurled insults at him and said, "You are this fellow's disciple! We are disciples of Moses! [29] We know that God spoke to Moses, but as for this fellow, we don't even know where he comes from."

[30] The man answered, "Now that is remarkable! You don't know where he comes from, yet he opened my eyes. [30] We know that God does not listen to sinners. He listens to the godly man who does his will. [32] Nobody has ever heard of opening the eyes of a man born blind. [33] If this man were not from God, he could do nothing."

[34] To this they replied, "You were steeped in sin at birth; how dare you lecture us!" And they threw him out.

[35] Jesus heard that they had thrown him out, and when he found him, he said, "Do you believe in the Son of Man?"

[36] "Who is he, sir?" the man asked. "Tell me so that I may believe in him."

[37] Jesus said, "You have now seen him; in fact, he is the one speaking with you."

[38] Then the man said, "Lord, I believe," and he worshiped him.

[39] Jesus said, "For judgment I have come into this world, so that the blind will see and those who see will become blind."

[40] Some Pharisees who were with him heard him say this and asked, "What? Are we blind too?"

[41] Jesus said, "If you were blind, you would not be guilty of sin; but now that you claim you can see, your guilt remains.

Chapter 10

[1] "I tell you the truth, the man who does not enter the sheep pen by the gate, but climbs in by some other way, is a thief and a robber. [2] The man who enters by the gate is the shepherd of his sheep. [3] The watchman opens the gate for him, and the sheep listen to his voice. He calls his own sheep by name and leads them out. [4] When he has brought out all his own, he goes on ahead of them, and his sheep follow him because they know his voice. [5] But they will never follow a stranger; in fact, they will run away from him because they do not recognize a stranger's voice." [6]

Jesus used this figure of speech, but they did not understand what he was telling them.

[7] Therefore Jesus said again, "I tell you the truth, I am the gate for the sheep. [8] All who ever came before me were thieves and robbers, but the sheep did not listen to them. [9] I am the gate; whoever enters through me will be saved. He will come in and go out, and find pasture. [10] The thief comes only to steal and kill and destroy; I have come that they may have life, and have it to the full.

[11] "I am the good shepherd. The good shepherd lays down his life for the sheep. [12] The hired hand is not the shepherd who owns the sheep. So when he sees the wolf coming, he abandons the sheep and runs away. Then the wolf attacks the flock and scatters it. [13] The man runs away because he is a hired hand and cares nothing for the sheep.

[14] "I am the good shepherd; I know my sheep and my sheep know me—[15] just as the Father knows me and I know the Father—and I lay down my life for the sheep. [16] I have other sheep that are not of this sheep pen. I must bring them also. They too will listen to my voice, and there shall be one flock and one shepherd. [17] The reason my Father loves me is that I lay down my life—only to take it up again. [18] No one takes it from me, but I lay it down of my own accord. I have authority to lay it down and authority to take it up again. This command I received from my Father."

[19] At these words the Jews were again divided. [20] Many of them said, "He is demon-possessed and raving mad. Why listen to him?"

[21] But others said, "These are not the sayings of a man possessed by a demon. Can a demon open the eyes of the blind?"

[22] Then came the Feast of Dedication at Jerusalem. It was winter, [23] and Jesus was in the temple area walking in Solomon's Colonnade. [24] The Jews gathered around him, saying, "How long will you keep us in suspense? If you are the Christ, tell us plainly."

[25] Jesus answered, "I did tell you, but you do not believe. The miracles I do in my Father's name speak for me, [26] but you do not believe because you are not my sheep. [27] My sheep listen to my voice; I know them, and they follow me. [28] I give them eternal life, and they shall never perish; no one can snatch them out of my hand. [29] My Father, who has given them to me, is greater than all; no one can snatch them out of my Father's hand. [30] I and the Father are one."

[30] Again the Jews picked up stones to stone him, [32] but Jesus said to them, "I have shown you many great miracles from the Father. For which of these do you stone me?"

[33] "We are not stoning you for any of these," replied the Jews, "but for blasphemy, because you, a mere man, claim to be God."

[34] Jesus answered them, "Is it not written in your Law, 'I have said you are gods'? [35] If he called them 'gods,' to whom the word of God came—and the Scripture cannot be broken—[36] what about the one whom the Father set apart as his very own and sent into the world? Why then do you accuse me of blasphemy because I said, 'I am God's Son'? [37] Do not believe me unless I do what my Father does. [38] But if I do it, even though you do not believe me, believe the miracles, that you may know and understand that the Father is in me, and I in the Father." [39] Again they tried to seize him, but he escaped their grasp.

[40] Then Jesus went back across the Jordan to the place where John had been baptizing in the early days. Here he stayed [41] and many people came to him. They said, "Though John never performed a miraculous sign, all that John said about this man was true." [42] And in that place many believed in Jesus.

Chapter 11

[1] Now a man named Lazarus was sick. He was from Bethany, the village of Mary and her sister Martha. [2] This Mary, whose brother Lazarus now lay sick, was the same one who poured perfume on the Lord and wiped his feet with her hair. [3] So the sisters sent word to Jesus, "Lord, the one you love is sick."

[4] When he heard this, Jesus said, "This sickness will not end in death. No, it is for God's glory so that God's Son may be glorified through it." [5] Jesus loved Martha and her sister and Lazarus. [6] Yet when he heard that Lazarus was sick, he stayed where he was two more days.

[7] Then he said to his disciples, "Let us go back to Judea."

[8] "But Rabbi," they said, "a short while ago the Jews tried to stone you, and yet you are going back there?"

[9] Jesus answered, "Are there not twelve hours of daylight? A man who walks by day will not stumble, for he sees by this world's light. [10] It is when he walks by night that he stumbles, for he has no light."

[11] After he had said this, he went on to tell them, "Our friend Lazarus has fallen asleep; but I am going there to wake him up."

[12] His disciples replied, "Lord, if he sleeps, he will get better." [13] Jesus had been speaking of his death, but his disciples thought he meant natural sleep.

[14] So then he told them plainly, "Lazarus is dead, [15] and for your sake I am glad I was not there, so that you may believe. But let us go to him."

[16] Then Thomas (called Didymus) said to the rest of the disciples, "Let us also go, that we may die with him."

[17] On his arrival, Jesus found that Lazarus had already been in the tomb for four days. [18] Bethany was less than two miles from Jerusalem, [19] and many Jews had come to Martha and Mary to comfort them in the loss of their brother. [20] When Martha heard that Jesus was coming, she went out to meet him, but Mary stayed at home.

[21] "Lord," Martha said to Jesus, "if you had been here, my brother would not have died. [22] But I know that even now God will give you whatever you ask."

[23] Jesus said to her, "Your brother will rise again."

[24] Martha answered, "I know he will rise again in the resurrection at the last day."

[25] Jesus said to her, "I am the resurrection and the life. He who believes in me will live, even though he dies; [26] and whoever lives and believes in me will never die. Do you believe this?"

[27] "Yes, Lord," she told him, "I believe that you are the Christ, the Son of God, who was to come into the world."

[28] And after she had said this, she went back and called her sister Mary aside. "The Teacher is here," she said, "and is asking for you." [29] When Mary heard this, she got up quickly and went to him. [30] Now Jesus had not yet entered the village, but was still at the place where Martha had met him. [30] When the Jews who had been with Mary in the house, comforting her, noticed how quickly she got up and went out, they followed her, supposing she was going to the tomb to mourn there.

[32] When Mary reached the place where Jesus was and saw him, she fell at his feet and said, "Lord, if you had been here, my brother would not have died."

[33] When Jesus saw her weeping, and the Jews who had come along with her also weeping, he was deeply moved in spirit and troubled. [34] "Where have you laid him?" he asked.

"Come and see, Lord," they replied.

[35] Jesus wept.

[36] Then the Jews said, "See how he loved him!"

[37] But some of them said, "Could not he who opened the eyes of the blind man have kept this man from dying?"

[38] Jesus, once more deeply moved, came to the tomb. It was a cave with a stone laid across the entrance. [39] "Take away the stone," he said.

"But, Lord," said Martha, the sister of the dead man, "by this time there is a bad odor, for he has been there four days."

[40] Then Jesus said, "Did I not tell you that if you believed, you would see the glory of God?"

[41] So they took away the stone. Then Jesus looked up and said, "Father, I thank you that you have heard me. [42] I knew that you always hear me, but I said this for the benefit of the people standing here, that they may believe that you sent me."

[43] When he had said this, Jesus called in a loud voice, "Lazarus, come out!" [44] The dead man came out, his hands and feet wrapped with strips of linen, and a cloth around his face.

Jesus said to them, "Take off the grave clothes and let him go."

[45] Therefore many of the Jews who had come to visit Mary, and had seen what Jesus did, put their faith in him. [46] But some of them went to the Pharisees and told them what Jesus had done. [47] Then the chief priests and the Pharisees called a meeting of the Sanhedrin.

"What are we accomplishing?" they asked. "Here is this man performing many miraculous signs. [48] If we let him go on like this, everyone will believe in him, and then the Romans will come and take away both our place and our nation."

[49] Then one of them, named Caiaphas, who was high priest that year, spoke up, "You know nothing at all! [50] You do not realize that it is better for you that one man die for the people than that the whole nation perish."

[51] He did not say this on his own, but as high priest that year he prophesied that Jesus would die for the Jewish nation, [52] and not only for that nation but also for the scattered children of God, to bring them together and make them one. [53] So from that day on they plotted to take his life.

[54] Therefore Jesus no longer moved about publicly among the Jews. Instead he withdrew to a region near the desert, to a village called Ephraim, where he stayed with his disciples.

[55] When it was almost time for the Jewish Passover, many went up from the country to Jerusalem for their ceremonial cleansing before the Passover. [56] They kept looking for Jesus, and as they stood in the temple area they asked one another, "What do you think? Isn't he coming to the Feast at all?" [57] But the chief priests and Pharisees had given orders that if anyone found out where Jesus was, he should report it so that they might arrest him.

Chapter 12

[1] Six days before the Passover, Jesus arrived at Bethany, where Lazarus lived, whom Jesus had raised from the dead. [2] Here a dinner was given in Jesus' honor. Martha served, while Lazarus was among those reclining at the table with him. [3] Then Mary took about a pint of pure nard, an expensive perfume; she poured it on Jesus' feet and wiped his feet with her hair. And the house was filled with the fragrance of the perfume.

[4] But one of his disciples, Judas Iscariot, who was later to betray him, objected, [5] "Why wasn't this perfume sold and the money given to the poor? It was worth a year's wages." [6] He did not say this because he cared about the poor but because he was a thief; as keeper of the money bag, he used to help himself to what was put into it.

[7] "Leave her alone," Jesus replied. "It was intended that she should save this perfume for the day of my burial. [8] You will always have the poor among you, but you will not always have me."

[9] Meanwhile a large crowd of Jews found out that Jesus was there and came, not only because of him but also to see Lazarus, whom he had raised from the dead. [10] So the chief priests made plans to kill Lazarus as well, [11] for on account of him many of the Jews were going over to Jesus and putting their faith in him.

[12] The next day the great crowd that had come for the Feast heard that Jesus was on his way to Jerusalem. [13] They took palm branches and went out to meet him, shouting,

"Hosanna!"

"Blessed is he who comes in the name of the Lord!"

"Blessed is the King of Israel!"

[14] Jesus found a young donkey and sat upon it, as it is written,

[15] "Do not be afraid, O Daughter of Zion;
see, your king is coming,
seated on a donkey's colt."

[16] At first his disciples did not understand all this. Only after Jesus was glorified did they realize that these things had been written about him and that they had done these things to him.

[17] Now the crowd that was with him when he called Lazarus from the tomb and raised him from the dead continued to spread the word. [18] Many people, because they had heard that he had given this miraculous sign, went out to meet him. [19] So the Pharisees said to one another, "See, this is getting us nowhere. Look how the whole world has gone after him!"

[20] Now there were some Greeks among those who went up to worship at the Feast. [21] They came to Philip, who was from Bethsaida in Galilee, with a request. "Sir," they said, "we would like to see Jesus." [22] Philip went to tell Andrew; Andrew and Philip in turn told Jesus.

[23] Jesus replied, "The hour has come for the Son of Man to be glorified. [24] I tell you the truth, unless a kernel of wheat falls to the ground and dies, it remains only a single seed. But if it dies, it produces many seeds. [25] The man who loves his life will lose it, while the man who hates his life in this world will keep it for eternal life. [26] Whoever serves me must follow me; and where I am, my servant also will be. My Father will honor the one who serves me.

[27] "Now my heart is troubled, and what shall I say? 'Father, save me from this hour'? No, it was for this very reason I came to this hour. [28] Father, glorify your name!"

Then a voice came from heaven, "I have glorified it, and will glorify it again." [29] The crowd that was there and heard it said it had thundered; others said an angel had spoken to him.

[30] Jesus said, "This voice was for your benefit, not mine. [30] Now is the time for judgment on this world; now the prince of this world will be driven out. [32] But I, when I am lifted up from the earth, will draw all men to myself." [33] He said this to show the kind of death he was going to die.

[34] The crowd spoke up, "We have heard from the Law that the Christ will remain forever, so how can you say, 'The Son of Man must be lifted up'? Who is this 'Son of Man'?"

[35] Then Jesus told them, "You are going to have the light just a little while longer. Walk while you have the light, before darkness overtakes you. The man who walks in the dark does not know where he is going. [36] Put your trust in the light while you have it, so that you may become sons of light." When he had finished speaking, Jesus left and hid himself from them.

[37] Even after Jesus had done all these miraculous signs in their presence, they still would not believe in him. [38] This was to fulfill the word of Isaiah the prophet:

"Lord, who has believed our message
and to whom has the arm of the Lord been revealed?"

[39] For this reason they could not believe, because, as Isaiah says elsewhere:

[40]   "He has blinded their eyes
and deadened their hearts,
so they can neither see with their eyes,

nor understand with their hearts,
nor turn—and I would heal them."

[41] Isaiah said this because he saw Jesus' glory and spoke about him.

[42] Yet at the same time many even among the leaders believed in him. But because of the Pharisees they would not confess their faith for fear they would be put out of the synagogue; [43] for they loved praise from men more than praise from God.

[44] Then Jesus cried out, "When a man believes in me, he does not believe in me only, but in the one who sent me. [45] When he looks at me, he sees the one who sent me. [46] I have come into the world as a light, so that no one who believes in me should stay in darkness.

[47] "As for the person who hears my words but does not keep them, I do not judge him. For I did not come to judge the world, but to save it. [48] There is a judge for the one who rejects me and does not accept my words; that very word which I spoke will condemn him at the last day. [49] For I did not speak of my own accord, but the Father who sent me commanded me what to say and how to say it. [50] I know that his command leads to eternal life. So whatever I say is just what the Father has told me to say."

Chapter 13

[1] It was just before the Passover Feast. Jesus knew that the time had come for him to leave this world and go to the Father. Having loved his own who were in the world, he now showed them the full extent of his love.

[2] The evening meal was being served, and the devil had already prompted Judas Iscariot, son of Simon, to betray Jesus. [3] Jesus knew that the Father had put all things under his power, and that he had come from God and was returning to God; [4] so he got up from the meal, took off his outer clothing, and wrapped a towel around his waist. [5] After that, he poured water into a basin and began to wash his disciples' feet, drying them with the towel that was wrapped around him.

[6] He came to Simon Peter, who said to him, "Lord, are you going to wash my feet?"

[7] Jesus replied, "You do not realize now what I am doing, but later you will understand."

[8] "No," said Peter, "you shall never wash my feet."

Jesus answered, "Unless I wash you, you have no part with me."

[9] "Then, Lord," Simon Peter replied, "not just my feet but my hands and my head as well!"

¹⁰ Jesus answered, "A person who has had a bath needs only to wash his feet; his whole body is clean. And you are clean, though not every one of you." ¹¹ For he knew who was going to betray him, and that was why he said not every one was clean.

¹² When he had finished washing their feet, he put on his clothes and returned to his place. "Do you understand what I have done for you?" he asked them. ¹³ "You call me 'Teacher' and 'Lord,' and rightly so, for that is what I am. ¹⁴ Now that I, your Lord and Teacher, have washed your feet, you also should wash one another's feet. ¹⁵ I have set you an example that you should do as I have done for you. ¹⁶ I tell you the truth, no servant is greater than his master, nor is a messenger greater than the one who sent him. ¹⁷ Now that you know these things, you will be blessed if you do them.

¹⁸ "I am not referring to all of you; I know those I have chosen. But this is to fulfill the scripture: 'He who shares my bread has lifted up his heel against me.'

¹⁹ "I am telling you now before it happens, so that when it does happen you will believe that I am He. ²⁰ I tell you the truth, whoever accepts anyone I send accepts me; and whoever accepts me accepts the one who sent me."

²¹ After he had said this, Jesus was troubled in spirit and testified, "I tell you the truth, one of you is going to betray me."

²² His disciples stared at one another, at a loss to know which of them he meant. ²³ One of them, the disciple whom Jesus loved, was reclining next to him. ²⁴ Simon Peter motioned to this disciple and said, "Ask him which one he means."

²⁵ Leaning back against Jesus, he asked him, "Lord, who is it?"

²⁶ Jesus answered, "It is the one to whom I will give this piece of bread when I have dipped it in the dish." Then, dipping the piece of bread, he gave it to Judas Iscariot, son of Simon. ²⁷ As soon as Judas took the bread, Satan entered into him.

"What you are about to do, do quickly," Jesus told him, ²⁸ but no one at the meal understood why Jesus said this to him. ²⁹ Since Judas had charge of the money, some thought Jesus was telling him to buy what was needed for the Feast, or to give something to the poor. ³⁰ As soon as Judas had taken the bread, he went out. And it was night.

³⁰ When he was gone, Jesus said, "Now is the Son of Man glorified and God is glorified in him. ³² If God is glorified in him, God will glorify the Son in himself, and will glorify him at once.

³³ "My children, I will be with you only a little longer. You will look for me, and just as I told the Jews, so I tell you now: Where I am going, you cannot come.

³⁴ "A new command I give you: Love one another. As I have loved you, so you must love one another. ³⁵ By this all men will know that you are my disciples, if you love one another."

³⁶ Simon Peter asked him, "Lord, where are you going?"

Jesus replied, "Where I am going, you cannot follow now, but you will follow later."

³⁷ Peter asked, "Lord, why can't I follow you now? I will lay down my life for you."

³⁸ Then Jesus answered, "Will you really lay down your life for me? I tell you the truth, before the rooster crows, you will disown me three times!

Chapter 14

¹ "Do not let your hearts be troubled. Trust in God; trust also in me. ² In my Father's house are many rooms; if it were not so, I would have told you. I am going there to prepare a place for you. ³ And if I go and prepare a place for you, I will come back and take you to be with me that you also may be where I am. ⁴ You know the way to the place where I am going."

⁵ Thomas said to him, "Lord, we don't know where you are going, so how can we know the way?"

⁶ Jesus answered, "I am the way and the truth and the life. No one comes to the Father except through me. ⁷ If you really knew me, you would know my Father as well. From now on, you do know him and have seen him."

⁸ Philip said, "Lord, show us the Father and that will be enough for us."

⁹ Jesus answered: "Don't you know me, Philip, even after I have been among you such a long time? Anyone who has seen me has seen the Father. How can you say, 'Show us the Father'? ¹⁰ Don't you believe that I am in the Father, and that the Father is in me? The words I say to you are not just my own. Rather, it is the Father, living in me, who is doing his work. ¹¹ Believe me when I say that I am in the Father and the Father is in me; or at least believe on the evidence of the miracles themselves. ¹² I tell you the truth, anyone who has faith in me will do what I have been doing. He will do even greater things than these, because I am going to the Father. ¹³ And I will do whatever you ask in my name, so that the Son may

bring glory to the Father. [14] You may ask me for anything in my name, and I will do it.

[15] "If you love me, you will obey what I command. [16] And I will ask the Father, and he will give you another Counselor to be with you forever—[17] the Spirit of truth. The world cannot accept him, because it neither sees him nor knows him. But you know him, for he lives with you and will be in you. [18] I will not leave you as orphans; I will come to you. [19] Before long, the world will not see me anymore, but you will see me. Because I live, you also will live. [20] On that day you will realize that I am in my Father, and you are in me, and I am in you. [21] Whoever has my commands and obeys them, he is the one who loves me. He who loves me will be loved by my Father, and I too will love him and show myself to him."

[22] Then Judas (not Judas Iscariot) said, "But, Lord, why do you intend to show yourself to us and not to the world?"

[23] Jesus replied, "If anyone loves me, he will obey my teaching. My Father will love him, and we will come to him and make our home with him. [24] He who does not love me will not obey my teaching. These words you hear are not my own; they belong to the Father who sent me.

[25] "All this I have spoken while still with you. [26] But the Counselor, the Holy Spirit, whom the Father will send in my name, will teach you all things and will remind you of everything I have said to you. [27] Peace I leave with you; my peace I give you. I do not give to you as the world gives. Do not let your hearts be troubled and do not be afraid.

[28] "You heard me say, 'I am going away and I am coming back to you.' If you loved me, you would be glad that I am going to the Father, for the Father is greater than I. [29] I have told you now before it happens, so that when it does happen you will believe. [30] I will not speak with you much longer, for the prince of this world is coming. He has no hold on me, [30] but the world must learn that I love the Father and that I do exactly what my Father has commanded me.

"Come now; let us leave."

Chapter 15

[1] "I am the true vine, and my Father is the gardener. [2] He cuts off every branch in me that bears no fruit, while every branch that does bear fruit he prunes so that it will be even more fruitful. [3] You are already clean because of the word I have spoken to you. [4] Remain in me, and I will remain in you. No branch can bear fruit by itself; it must remain in the vine. Neither can you bear fruit unless you remain in me.

[5] "I am the vine; you are the branches. If a man remains in me and I in him, he will bear much fruit; apart from me you can do nothing. [6] If

anyone does not remain in me, he is like a branch that is thrown away and withers; such branches are picked up, thrown into the fire and burned. [7] If you remain in me and my words remain in you, ask whatever you wish, and it will be given you. [8] This is to my Father's glory, that you bear much fruit, showing yourselves to be my disciples.

[9] "As the Father has loved me, so have I loved you. Now remain in my love. [10] If you obey my commands, you will remain in my love, just as I have obeyed my Father's commands and remain in his love. [11] I have told you this so that my joy may be in you and that your joy may be complete. [12] My command is this: Love each other as I have loved you. [13] Greater love has no one than this, that he lay down his life for his friends. [14] You are my friends if you do what I command. [15] I no longer call you servants, because a servant does not know his master's business. Instead, I have called you friends, for everything that I learned from my Father I have made known to you. [16] You did not choose me, but I chose you and appointed you to go and bear fruit—fruit that will last. Then the Father will give you whatever you ask in my name. [17] This is my command: Love each other.

[18] "If the world hates you, keep in mind that it hated me first. [19] If you belonged to the world, it would love you as its own. As it is, you do not belong to the world, but I have chosen you out of the world. That is why the world hates you. [20] Remember the words I spoke to you: 'No servant is greater than his master.' If they persecuted me, they will persecute you also. If they obeyed my teaching, they will obey yours also. [21] They will treat you this way because of my name, for they do not know the One who sent me. [22] If I had not come and spoken to them, they would not be guilty of sin. Now, however, they have no excuse for their sin. [23] He who hates me hates my Father as well. [24] If I had not done among them what no one else did, they would not be guilty of sin. But now they have seen these miracles, and yet they have hated both me and my Father. [25] But this is to fulfill what is written in their Law: 'They hated me without reason.'

[26] "When the Counselor comes, whom I will send to you from the Father, the Spirit of truth who goes out from the Father, he will testify about me. [27] And you also must testify, for you have been with me from the beginning.

Chapter 16

[1] "All this I have told you so that you will not go astray. [2] They will put you out of the synagogue; in fact, a time is coming when anyone who kills you will think he is offering a service to God. [3] They will do such things because they have not known the Father or me. [4] I have told you

this, so that when the time comes you will remember that I warned you. I did not tell you this at first because I was with you.

⁵ "Now I am going to him who sent me, yet none of you asks me, 'Where are you going?' ⁶ Because I have said these things, you are filled with grief. ⁷ But I tell you the truth: It is for your good that I am going away. Unless I go away, the Counselor will not come to you; but if I go, I will send him to you. ⁸ When he comes, he will convict the world of guilt in regard to sin and righteousness and judgment: ⁹ in regard to sin, because men do not believe in me; ¹⁰ in regard to righteousness, because I am going to the Father, where you can see me no longer; ¹¹ and in regard to judgment, because the prince of this world now stands condemned.

¹² "I have much more to say to you, more than you can now bear. ¹³ But when he, the Spirit of truth, comes, he will guide you into all truth. He will not speak on his own; he will speak only what he hears, and he will tell you what is yet to come. ¹⁴ He will bring glory to me by taking from what is mine and making it known to you. ¹⁵ All that belongs to the Father is mine. That is why I said the Spirit will take from what is mine and make it known to you.

¹⁶ "In a little while you will see me no more, and then after a little while you will see me."

¹⁷ Some of his disciples said to one another, "What does he mean by saying, 'In a little while you will see me no more, and then after a little while you will see me,' and 'Because I am going to the Father'?" ¹⁸ They kept asking, "What does he mean by 'a little while'? We don't understand what he is saying."

¹⁹ Jesus saw that they wanted to ask him about this, so he said to them, "Are you asking one another what I meant when I said, 'In a little while you will see me no more, and then after a little while you will see me'? ²⁰ I tell you the truth, you will weep and mourn while the world rejoices. You will grieve, but your grief will turn to joy. ²¹ A woman giving birth to a child has pain because her time has come; but when her baby is born she forgets the anguish because of her joy that a child is born into the world. ²² So with you: Now is your time of grief, but I will see you again and you will rejoice, and no one will take away your joy. ²³ In that day you will no longer ask me anything. I tell you the truth, my Father will give you whatever you ask in my name. ²⁴ Until now you have not asked for anything in my name. Ask and you will receive, and your joy will be complete.

²⁵ "Though I have been speaking figuratively, a time is coming when I will no longer use this kind of language but will tell you plainly about my Father. ²⁶ In that day you will ask in my name. I am not saying that I will

ask the Father on your behalf. [27] No, the Father himself loves you because you have loved me and have believed that I came from God. [28] I came from the Father and entered the world; now I am leaving the world and going back to the Father."

[29] Then Jesus' disciples said, "Now you are speaking clearly and without figures of speech. [30] Now we can see that you know all things and that you do not even need to have anyone ask you questions. This makes us believe that you came from God."

[30] "You believe at last!" Jesus answered. [32] "But a time is coming, and has come, when you will be scattered, each to his own home. You will leave me all alone. Yet I am not alone, for my Father is with me.

[33] "I have told you these things, so that in me you may have peace. In this world you will have trouble. But take heart! I have overcome the world."

Chapter 17

[1] After Jesus said this, he looked toward heaven and prayed:

"Father, the time has come. Glorify your Son, that your Son may glorify you. [2] For you granted him authority over all people that he might give eternal life to all those you have given him. [3] Now this is eternal life: that they may know you, the only true God, and Jesus Christ, whom you have sent. [4] I have brought you glory on earth by completing the work you gave me to do. [5] And now, Father, glorify me in your presence with the glory I had with you before the world began.

[6] "I have revealed you to those whom you gave me out of the world. They were yours; you gave them to me and they have obeyed your word. [7] Now they know that everything you have given me comes from you. [8] For I gave them the words you gave me and they accepted them. They knew with certainty that I came from you, and they believed that you sent me. [9] I pray for them. I am not praying for the world, but for those you have given me, for they are yours. [10] All I have is yours, and all you have is mine. And glory has come to me through them. [11] I will remain in the world no longer, but they are still in the world, and I am coming to you. Holy Father, protect them by the power of your name—the name you gave me—so that they may be one as we are one. [12] While I was with them, I protected them and kept them safe by that name you gave me. None has been lost except the one doomed to destruction so that Scripture would be fulfilled.

[13] "I am coming to you now, but I say these things while I am still in the world, so that they may have the full measure of my joy within them. [14] I have given them your word and the world has hated them, for they are not of the world any more than I am of the world. [15] My prayer is not that you take them out of the world but that you protect them from the evil one. [16] They are not of the world, even as I am not of it. [17] Sanctify them by the truth; your word is truth. [18] As you sent me into the world, I have sent them into the world. [19] For them I sanctify myself, that they too may be truly sanctified.

[20] "My prayer is not for them alone. I pray also for those who will believe in me through their message, [21] that all of them may be one, Father, just as you are in me and I am in you. May they also be in us so that the world may believe that you have sent me. [22] I have given them the glory that you gave me, that they may be one as we are one: [23] I in them and you in me. May they be brought to complete unity to let the world know that you sent me and have loved them even as you have loved me.

[24] "Father, I want those you have given me to be with me where I am, and to see my glory, the glory you have given me because you loved me before the creation of the world.

[25] "Righteous Father, though the world does not know you, I know you, and they know that you have sent me. [26] I have made you known to them, and will continue to make you known in order that the love you have for me may be in them and that I myself may be in them."

Chapter 18

[1] When he had finished praying, Jesus left with his disciples and crossed the Kidron Valley. On the other side there was an olive grove, and he and his disciples went into it.

[2] Now Judas, who betrayed him, knew the place, because Jesus had often met there with his disciples. [3] So Judas came to the grove, guiding a detachment of soldiers and some officials from the chief priests and Pharisees. They were carrying torches, lanterns and weapons.

[4] Jesus, knowing all that was going to happen to him, went out and asked them, "Who is it you want?"

[5] "Jesus of Nazareth," they replied.

"I am he," Jesus said. (And Judas the traitor was standing there with them.) [6] When Jesus said, "I am he," they drew back and fell to the ground.

[7] Again he asked them, "Who is it you want?"

And they said, "Jesus of Nazareth."

[8] "I told you that I am he," Jesus answered. "If you are looking for me, then let these men go." [9] This happened so that the words he had spoken would be fulfilled: "I have not lost one of those you gave me."

[10] Then Simon Peter, who had a sword, drew it and struck the high priest's servant, cutting off his right ear. (The servant's name was Malchus.)

[11] Jesus commanded Peter, "Put your sword away! Shall I not drink the cup the Father has given me?"

[12] Then the detachment of soldiers with its commander and the Jewish officials arrested Jesus. They bound him [13] and brought him first to Annas, who was the father-in-law of Caiaphas, the high priest that year. [14] Caiaphas was the one who had advised the Jews that it would be good if one man died for the people.

[15] Simon Peter and another disciple were following Jesus. Because this disciple was known to the high priest, he went with Jesus into the high priest's courtyard, [16] but Peter had to wait outside at the door. The other disciple, who was known to the high priest, came back, spoke to the girl on duty there and brought Peter in.

[17] "You are not one of his disciples, are you?" the girl at the door asked Peter.

He replied, "I am not."

[18] It was cold, and the servants and officials stood around a fire they had made to keep warm. Peter also was standing with them, warming himself.

[19] Meanwhile, the high priest questioned Jesus about his disciples and his teaching.

[20] "I have spoken openly to the world," Jesus replied. "I always taught in synagogues or at the temple, where all the Jews come together. I said nothing in secret. [21] Why question me? Ask those who heard me. Surely they know what I said."

[22] When Jesus said this, one of the officials nearby struck him in the face. "Is this the way you answer the high priest?" he demanded.

[23] "If I said something wrong," Jesus replied, "testify as to what is wrong. But if I spoke the truth, why did you strike me?" [24] Then Annas sent him, still bound, to Caiaphas the high priest.

[25] As Simon Peter stood warming himself, he was asked, "You are not one of his disciples, are you?"

He denied it, saying, "I am not."

²⁶ One of the high priest's servants, a relative of the man whose ear Peter had cut off, challenged him, "Didn't I see you with him in the olive grove?" ²⁷ Again Peter denied it, and at that moment a rooster began to crow.

²⁸ Then the Jews led Jesus from Caiaphas to the palace of the Roman governor. By now it was early morning, and to avoid ceremonial uncleanness the Jews did not enter the palace; they wanted to be able to eat the Passover. ²⁹ So Pilate came out to them and asked, "What charges are you bringing against this man?"

³⁰ "If he were not a criminal," they replied, "we would not have handed him over to you."

³⁰ Pilate said, "Take him yourselves and judge him by your own law."

"But we have no right to execute anyone," the Jews objected. ³² This happened so that the words Jesus had spoken indicating the kind of death he was going to die would be fulfilled.

³³ Pilate then went back inside the palace, summoned Jesus and asked him, "Are you the king of the Jews?"

³⁴ "Is that your own idea," Jesus asked, "or did others talk to you about me?"

³⁵ "Am I a Jew?" Pilate replied. "It was your people and your chief priests who handed you over to me. What is it you have done?"

³⁶ Jesus said,

"My kingdom is not of this world. If it were, my servants would fight to prevent my arrest by the Jews. But now my kingdom is from another place." ³⁷ "You are a king, then!" said Pilate.

Jesus answered, "You are right in saying I am a king. In fact, for this reason I was born, and for this I came into the world, to testify to the truth. Everyone on the side of truth listens to me."

³⁸ "What is truth?" Pilate asked. With this he went out again to the Jews and said, "I find no basis for a charge against him. ³⁹ But it is your custom for me to release to you one prisoner at the time of the Passover. Do you want me to release 'the king of the Jews'?"

⁴⁰ They shouted back, "No, not him! Give us Barabbas!" Now Barabbas had taken part in a rebellion.

Chapter 19

¹ Then Pilate took Jesus and had him flogged. ² The soldiers twisted together a crown of thorns and put it on his head. They clothed him in a purple robe ³ and went up to him again and again, saying, "Hail, king of the Jews!" And they struck him in the face.

[4] Once more Pilate came out and said to the Jews, "Look, I am bringing him out to you to let you know that I find no basis for a charge against him." [5] When Jesus came out wearing the crown of thorns and the purple robe, Pilate said to them, "Here is the man!"

[6] As soon as the chief priests and their officials saw him, they shouted, "Crucify! Crucify!"

But Pilate answered, "You take him and crucify him. As for me, I find no basis for a charge against him."

[7] The Jews insisted, "We have a law, and according to that law he must die, because he claimed to be the Son of God."

[8] When Pilate heard this, he was even more afraid, [9] and he went back inside the palace. "Where do you come from?" he asked Jesus, but Jesus gave him no answer. [10] "Do you refuse to speak to me?" Pilate said. "Don't you realize I have power either to free you or to crucify you?"

[11] Jesus answered, "You would have no power over me if it were not given to you from above. Therefore the one who handed me over to you is guilty of a greater sin."

[12] From then on, Pilate tried to set Jesus free, but the Jews kept shouting, "If you let this man go, you are no friend of Caesar. Anyone who claims to be a king opposes Caesar."

[13] When Pilate heard this, he brought Jesus out and sat down on the judge's seat at a place known as the Stone Pavement (which in Aramaic is Gabbatha). [14] It was the day of Preparation of Passover Week, about the sixth hour.

"Here is your king," Pilate said to the Jews.

[15] But they shouted, "Take him away! Take him away! Crucify him!"

"Shall I crucify your king?" Pilate asked.

"We have no king but Caesar," the chief priests answered.

[16] Finally Pilate handed him over to them to be crucified.

So the soldiers took charge of Jesus. [17] Carrying his own cross, he went out to the place of the Skull (which in Aramaic is called Golgotha). [18] Here they crucified him, and with him two others—one on each side and Jesus in the middle.

[19] Pilate had a notice prepared and fastened to the cross. It read: JESUS OF NAZARETH, THE KING OF THE JEWS. [20] Many of the Jews read this sign, for the place where Jesus was crucified was near the city, and the sign was written in Aramaic, Latin and Greek. [21] The chief priests of the Jews protested to Pilate, "Do not write 'The King of the Jews,' but that this man claimed to be king of the Jews."

²² Pilate answered, "What I have written, I have written."

²³ When the soldiers crucified Jesus, they took his clothes, dividing them into four shares, one for each of them, with the undergarment remaining. This garment was seamless, woven in one piece from top to bottom. ²⁴ "Let's not tear it," they said to one another. "Let's decide by lot who will get it."

This happened that the scripture might be fulfilled which said,

"They divided my garments among them
and cast lots for my clothing."

So this is what the soldiers did.

²⁵ Near the cross of Jesus stood his mother, his mother's sister, Mary the wife of Clopas, and Mary Magdalene. ²⁶ When Jesus saw his mother there, and the disciple whom he loved standing nearby, he said to his mother, "Dear woman, here is your son," ²⁷ and to the disciple, "Here is your mother." From that time on, this disciple took her into his home.

²⁸ Later, knowing that all was now completed, and so that the Scripture would be fulfilled, Jesus said, "I am thirsty." ²⁹ A jar of wine vinegar was there, so they soaked a sponge in it, put the sponge on a stalk of the hyssop plant, and lifted it to Jesus' lips. ³⁰ When he had received the drink, Jesus said, "It is finished." With that, he bowed his head and gave up his spirit.

³⁰ Now it was the day of Preparation, and the next day was to be a special Sabbath. Because the Jews did not want the bodies left on the crosses during the Sabbath, they asked Pilate to have the legs broken and the bodies taken down. ³² The soldiers therefore came and broke the legs of the first man who had been crucified with Jesus, and then those of the other. ³³ But when they came to Jesus and found that he was already dead, they did not break his legs. ³⁴ Instead, one of the soldiers pierced Jesus' side with a spear, bringing a sudden flow of blood and water. ³⁵ The man who saw it has given testimony, and his testimony is true. He knows that he tells the truth, and he testifies so that you also may believe. ³⁶ These things happened so that the scripture would be fulfilled: "Not one of his bones will be broken," ³⁷ and, as another scripture says, "They will look on the one they have pierced."

³⁸ Later, Joseph of Arimathea asked Pilate for the body of Jesus. Now Joseph was a disciple of Jesus, but secretly because he feared the Jews. With Pilate's permission, he came and took the body away. ³⁹ He was accompanied by Nicodemus, the man who earlier had visited Jesus at night. Nicodemus brought a mixture of myrrh and aloes, about seventy-five

pounds. [40] Taking Jesus' body, the two of them wrapped it, with the spices, in strips of linen. This was in accordance with Jewish burial customs. [41] At the place where Jesus was crucified, there was a garden, and in the garden a new tomb, in which no one had ever been laid. [42] Because it was the Jewish day of Preparation and since the tomb was nearby, they laid Jesus there.

Chapter 20

[1] Early on the first day of the week, while it was still dark, Mary Magdalene went to the tomb and saw that the stone had been removed from the entrance. [2] So she came running to Simon Peter and the other disciple, the one Jesus loved, and said, "They have taken the Lord out of the tomb, and we don't know where they have put him!"

[3] So Peter and the other disciple started for the tomb. [4] Both were running, but the other disciple outran Peter and reached the tomb first. [5] He bent over and looked in at the strips of linen lying there but did not go in. [6] Then Simon Peter, who was behind him, arrived and went into the tomb. He saw the strips of linen lying there, [7] as well as the burial cloth that had been around Jesus' head. The cloth was folded up by itself, separate from the linen. [8] Finally the other disciple, who had reached the tomb first, also went inside. He saw and believed. [9] (They still did not understand from Scripture that Jesus had to rise from the dead.)

[10] Then the disciples went back to their homes, [11] but Mary stood outside the tomb crying. As she wept, she bent over to look into the tomb [12] and saw two angels in white, seated where Jesus' body had been, one at the head and the other at the foot.

[13] They asked her, "Woman, why are you crying?"

"They have taken my Lord away," she said, "and I don't know where they have put him." [14] At this, she turned around and saw Jesus standing there, but she did not realize that it was Jesus.

[15] "Woman," he said, "why are you crying? Who is it you are looking for?"

Thinking he was the gardener, she said, "Sir, if you have carried him away, tell me where you have put him, and I will get him."

[16] Jesus said to her, "Mary."

She turned toward him and cried out in Aramaic, "Rabboni!" (which means Teacher).

[17] Jesus said, "Do not hold on to me, for I have not yet returned to the Father. Go instead to my brothers and tell them, 'I am returning to my Father and your Father, to my God and your God.'"

[18] Mary Magdalene went to the disciples with the news: "I have seen the Lord!" And she told them that he had said these things to her.

[19] On the evening of that first day of the week, when the disciples were together, with the doors locked for fear of the Jews, Jesus came and stood among them and said, "Peace be with you!" [20] After he said this, he showed them his hands and side. The disciples were overjoyed when they saw the Lord.

[21] Again Jesus said, "Peace be with you! As the Father has sent me, I am sending you." [22] And with that he breathed on them and said, "Receive the Holy Spirit. [23] If you forgive anyone his sins, they are forgiven; if you do not forgive them, they are not forgiven."

[24] Now Thomas (called Didymus), one of the Twelve, was not with the disciples when Jesus came. [25] So the other disciples told him, "We have seen the Lord!"

But he said to them, "Unless I see the nail marks in his hands and put my finger where the nails were, and put my hand into his side, I will not believe it."

[26] A week later his disciples were in the house again, and Thomas was with them. Though the doors were locked, Jesus came and stood among them and said, "Peace be with you!" [27] Then he said to Thomas, "Put your finger here; see my hands. Reach out your hand and put it into my side. Stop doubting and believe."

[28] Thomas said to him, "My Lord and my God!"

[29] Then Jesus told him, "Because you have seen me, you have believed; blessed are those who have not seen and yet have believed."

[30] Jesus did many other miraculous signs in the presence of his disciples, which are not recorded in this book. [31] But these are written that you may believe that Jesus is the Christ, the Son of God, and that by believing you may have life in his name.

Chapter 21

[1] Afterward Jesus appeared again to his disciples, by the Sea of Tiberias. It happened this way: [2] Simon Peter, Thomas (called Didymus), Nathanael from Cana in Galilee, the sons of Zebedee, and two other disciples were together. [3] "I'm going out to fish," Simon Peter told them, and they said, "We'll go with you." So they went out and got into the boat, but that night they caught nothing.

[4] Early in the morning, Jesus stood on the shore, but the disciples did not realize that it was Jesus.

[5] He called out to them, "Friends, haven't you any fish?"

"No," they answered.

[6] He said, "Throw your net on the right side of the boat and you will find some." When they did, they were unable to haul the net in because of the large number of fish.

[7] Then the disciple whom Jesus loved said to Peter, "It is the Lord!" As soon as Simon Peter heard him say, "It is the Lord," he wrapped his outer garment around him (for he had taken it off) and jumped into the water. [8] The other disciples followed in the boat, towing the net full of fish, for they were not far from shore, about a hundred yards. [9] When they landed, they saw a fire of burning coals there with fish on it, and some bread.

[10] Jesus said to them, "Bring some of the fish you have just caught."

[11] Simon Peter climbed aboard and dragged the net ashore. It was full of large fish, [153] , but even with so many the net was not torn. [12] Jesus said to them, "Come and have breakfast." None of the disciples dared ask him, "Who are you?" They knew it was the Lord. [13] Jesus came, took the bread and gave it to them, and did the same with the fish. [14] This was now the third time Jesus appeared to his disciples after he was raised from the dead.

[15] When they had finished eating, Jesus said to Simon Peter, "Simon son of John, do you truly love me more than these?"

"Yes, Lord," he said, "you know that I love you."

Jesus said, "Feed my lambs."

[16] Again Jesus said, "Simon son of John, do you truly love me?"

He answered, "Yes, Lord, you know that I love you."

Jesus said, "Take care of my sheep."

[17] The third time he said to him, "Simon son of John, do you love me?"

Peter was hurt because Jesus asked him the third time, "Do you love me?" He said, "Lord, you know all things; you know that I love you."

Jesus said, "Feed my sheep. [18] I tell you the truth, when you were younger you dressed yourself and went where you wanted; but when you are old you will stretch out your hands, and someone else will dress you and lead you where you do not want to go." [19] Jesus said this to indicate the kind of death by which Peter would glorify God. Then he said to him, "Follow me!"

[20] Peter turned and saw that the disciple whom Jesus loved was following them. (This was the one who had leaned back against Jesus at the

supper and had said, "Lord, who is going to betray you?") [21] When Peter saw him, he asked, "Lord, what about him?"

[22] Jesus answered, "If I want him to remain alive until I return, what is that to you? You must follow me." [23] Because of this, the rumor spread among the brothers that this disciple would not die. But Jesus did not say that he would not die; he only said, "If I want him to remain alive until I return, what is that to you?"

[24] This is the disciple who testifies to these things and who wrote them down. We know that his testimony is true.

[25] Jesus did many other things as well. If every one of them were written down, I suppose that even the whole world would not have room for the books that would be written.